OUR

TWELVE

STEPS

◆

Members share how AA's Twelve Steps
have changed their lives

AAGRAPEVINE,Inc.

New York, New York
WWW. AAGRAPEVINE.ORG

OUR

TWELVE

STEPS

———◆———

Members share how AA's Twelve Steps
have changed their lives

BOOKS PUBLISHED BY AA GRAPEVINE, INC.

The Language of the Heart (& eBook)
The Best of the Grapevine Volumes I, II, III
The Best of Bill (& eBook)
Thank You for Sharing
Spiritual Awakenings I & II (& eBooks)
I Am Responsible: The Hand of AA
Emotional Sobriety I & II—The Next Frontier (& eBooks)
In Our Own Words: Stories of Young AAs in Recovery (& eBook)
Beginners' Book (& eBook)
Voices of Long-Term Sobriety (& eBook)
A Rabbit Walks Into A Bar
Step by Step—Real AAs, Real Recovery (& eBook)
Young & Sober (& eBook)
Into Action (& eBook)
Happy, Joyous & Free (& eBook)
One on One (& eBook)
No Matter What (& eBook)
Grapevine Daily Quote Book (& eBook)
Sober & Out (& eBook)
Forming True Partnerships (& eBook)
Our Twelve Traditions (& eBook)
Making Amends (& eBook)
Voices of Women in AA (& eBook)
AA in the Military (& eBook)
One Big Tent (& eBook)
Take Me to Your Sponsor (& eBook)
Free on the Inside (& eBook)
Prayer & Meditation (& eBook)
Fun in Sobriety (& eBook)
The Home Group: Heartbeat of AA-30th Anniversary Ed. (& eBook)

IN SPANISH

El lenguaje del corazón
Lo mejor de Bill (& eBook)
El grupo base: Corazón de AA
Lo mejor de La Viña
Felices, alegres y libres (& eBook)
Un día a la vez (& eBook)
Frente A Frente (& eBook)
Bajo El Mismo Techo (& eBook)
Sobriedad emocional (& eBook)

IN FRENCH

Le langage du coeur
Les meilleurs articles de Bill
*Le Groupe d'attache: Le battement
du coeur des AA*
En tête à tête (& eBook)
Heureux, joyeux et libres (& eBook)
La sobriété émotive

AA PREAMBLE

Alcoholics Anonymous is a fellowship of people who
share their experience, strength and hope
with each other that they may solve their common problem
and help others to recover from alcoholism.

The only requirement for membership is a desire to stop drinking.
There are no dues or fees for AA membership;
we are self-supporting through our own contributions.
AA is not allied with any sect, denomination, politics, organization
or institution; does not wish to engage in any controversy,
neither endorses nor opposes any causes.

Our primary purpose is to stay sober
and help other alcoholics to achieve sobriety.

©AA Grapevine, Inc.

Contents

INTRODUCTION: A LIFETIME PRACTICE

Members share how AA's Twelve Steps have changed their lives.

STEP ONE

We admitted we were powerless over alcohol—that our lives had become unmanageable.

STEP TWO

Came to believe that a Power greater than ourselves could restore us to sanity.

STEP THREE

Made a decision to turn our will and our lives over to the care of God *as we understood Him.*

STEP FOUR

Made a searching and fearless moral inventory of ourselves.

STEP FIVE

Admitted to God, to ourselves, and to another human being the exact nature of our wrongs.

STEP SIX

Were entirely ready to have God remove all these defects of character.

STEP SEVEN

Humbly asked Him to remove our shortcomings.

STEP EIGHT

Made a list of all persons we had harmed, and became willing to make amends to them all.

STEP NINE

Made direct amends to such people wherever possible, except when to do so would injure them or others.

STEP TEN

Continued to take personal inventory and when we were wrong promptly admitted it.

STEP ELEVEN

Sought through prayer and meditation to improve our conscious contact with God *as we understood Him,* praying only for knowledge of His will for us and the power to carry that out.

STEP TWELVE

Having had a spiritual awakening as the result of these steps, we tried to carry this message to alcoholics, and to practice these principles in all our affairs.

Welcome

One night in 1938, as AA cofounder Bill W. sat in a Brooklyn brownstone writing the book that became *Alcoholics Anonymous* (lovingly known by AA members as the Big Book), he came to a chapter that he entitled "How It Works."

And here, he paused. How would he explain to despairing alcoholics exactly how they would be able to find sobriety?

The answer, which Bill scrawled on the yellow paper tablets he composed on, became AA's Twelve Steps. Loosely based on four precepts of the Oxford Group, the Steps would forever change the face of recovery from alcoholism.

The first book of Step stories from AA Grapevine in more than a dozen years, *Our Twelve Steps* features fresh, up to date experiences from members who have seen and felt firsthand how the Steps can transform our lives while taking us on the path to sobriety. Removing alcohol; finding and improving a spiritual connection; examining the issues that kept us drinking; becoming honest with others; and reaching out to help fellow alcoholics is, as Mitchell K. writes in his insightful story "No Finish Line," "a manual for a life ... free of alcohol (or any other behaviors which keep me from living life to its fullest)."

In these stories, all of which originally appeared in Grapevine, alcoholics of all ages and backgrounds describe their personal experiences with the power of the Steps—lives knitted back together, relationships rebuilt, dreams revisited. They are central to sobriety in AA and to helping our fellow suffering alcoholics. As AA cofounder Dr. Bob wrote in what would be his last address to AA in 1950: "Our Twelve Steps, when simmered down to the last, resolve themselves into the words love and service."

INTRODUCTION:
A LIFETIME PRACTICE

———————◆———————

A phrase commonly used in AA is that a person is "working" the Steps, which implies rolled up sleeves and big pots of coffee (and there is a little of that!). But there is also the sense in many AAs in which, after we study them and do them, the Steps continue to work us. From the moment an alcoholic decides to quit drinking to the day they volunteer to help another alcoholic get sober, the Steps inform our actions. They represent a progression through sobriety, a way to interpret the world and one's own place in it without the distorting prism of alcohol. "My journey with the Steps continues," Dwight H. writes in "12 Reasons To Stay." "I perceive things differently now. When I'm restless, irritable and discontent, I have spiritual tools to use." Ultimately, the stories in this introductory chapter illustrate how AA's Twelve Steps provide everyone, newcomers and oldtimers alike, with a practical and spiritual roadmap for continued recovery from alcoholism.

A Treasure to Be Shared

July 2023

There's nothing I like more than sponsoring a woman who's willing to do the work in order to live a sober, happy life. My joy and my gift is to guide her through our Steps just like I was guided by my own sponsors.

I remember one day asking my sponsor in early sobriety, "When will I get to be a sponsor?" Her answer? "When God thinks you're ready."

I had finished my Steps the first year, but I was so busy with my own life and recovery at that time—a young family and my teaching career—that I had little time to spare. That changed a short while later when I took on my first sponsee.

Funny how helping another alcoholic puts life into perspective. My first sponsee came to my house on a Saturday, having read "The Doctor's Opinion," the chapter on Step One in the "Twelve and Twelve" and Chapters 2 and 3 in the Big Book. She had listed three specific incidents for each person in her life regarding how her drinking had affected them.

Yes, I had given her a lot of work to prepare for our meeting, but a busy alcoholic immersed in our literature has less time to think about taking a drink. I must have called my sponsor a hundred times asking her whether I was doing sponsorship right. This memory makes me smile. A sponsee is a fragile gift and I was just beginning to feel the honor of this trusted connection with another human being.

Twenty-eight years later, this trail of stars, bright faces of sponsees then and now, warms my soul and sustains my sobriety. Each one has taken me back to the scared mess I was when I got to my first AA meeting—sacred ground.

My sponsees have reminded me of that first year when I thought I'd never stop crying. When I share with them my embarrassing stories about inappropriate places I "relieved" myself as a drunk, I see the shame fall from the eyes of the women sitting across from me. We get to have a good laugh at ourselves. Each time I listen to a Fourth Step, my bond with a Higher Power deepens and so does my faith. The holy process of listening intently to another alcoholic stays with me for days. This road map of life we call the Steps is a treasure meant to be shared with those who want it. It reminds me of how blessed I am.

Recently a sponsee and I sat at my dining room table discussing Step Ten and the importance of cleaning up our defects daily so we can be useful to others. I emphasized the parts in the "Twelve and Twelve" that mention noting those things we've done well each day. Most of us are so good at focusing on the negative, but we can train ourselves to see the positive if we make it a practice.

My sobriety date is July 27, 1988. When I joined AA, I just wanted to stop drinking. In the process of doing the Steps the first time, I learned the importance of feeding and developing my spiritual life. I continue to do that by being grateful that I get to watch women transform their lives by working one Step at a time under the grace of a loving Higher Power.

Cynthia F.
Rancho Murieta, California

No Finish Line
June 2013

Over the past 20 years I have heard people state at meetings that they "did" the Steps or that they're working "through" the Steps. When put in this light, it sounds as though there's a definite goal to be obtained to which there's an end result. My experience is different. I've found that I'm never finished with the Steps, for they provide a structure for me to live by. Before AA, I had no chance for a happy and purposeful life. My old, self-imposed guidelines on how to live ended in despair and deprivation.

I experience the Steps daily; I can be working any one of them at any particular moment of the day. Gratefully, I don't see them as something to be endured or used as a means to an end. They're not unlike a manual for a life, to be free of alcohol (or any other behaviors which keep me from living life to its fullest).

Were the Steps merely a one-time event, I'm certain I'd be short-changing myself, for a part of me is a creature of habit. If I'm not constantly practicing healthy and productive life skills on a daily basis, I'll revert to my old coping skills, which will keep me imprisoned by my insane thinking and behaviors.

So rather than "doing" the Steps, I strive to make them an integral part of my being; a platform upon which I can live in tandem with the rhythm of life. It's a way I can experience the joy of living.

Mitchell K.
Philadelphia, Pennsylvania

12 Reasons to Stay
September 2023

We've prayed and completed the readings. The announcements have been made and now it's time for the breakout group. It's our Tuesday night Step study. This group goes through our *Twelve Steps and Twelve Traditions* book over and over again. I've been attending this meeting for years.

The room is filled and there's a lot of laughter and talk. This is my home group and I'm surrounded by friends, some I've known for years.

I've been attending literature meetings for four decades. I used to puzzle over how my grandfather could go to a Bible study for 60 years and not get bored. Now, I know. There are always more depths to plumb. I've learned that sometimes words and sentences jump off the page only when I'm ready to hear them and that someone else's perspective can open new worlds to me.

I love our cofounder Bill W.'s writing in our "Twelve and Twelve."

What I've noticed in the last few trips through the book is how he shows us the progression of sobriety in each Step. He takes us through a journey from dying and insanity to a sense of belonging and the joy of good living. His words parallel my own journey. He starts us out in Step One with words like "bankrupt," "complete defeat" and "merciless obsession." The goal, he says, is to "become as open-minded to conviction and as willing to listen as the dying can be."

I vividly remember the night in 1980 when I realized both that I was going to die if I kept drinking and that I couldn't stop on my own. I was terrified. Defiance, confusion and irrationality are key concepts at the core of Step Two. When I came into the program I was given the choice between an Arkansas prison and a treatment center. I couldn't decide. That's how insane I had become. My attorney finally convinced me to go to treatment, telling me that prison could be arranged for me later if I still wanted that.

Willingness is the key to the Third Step. On that night when I realized I was dying from alcoholism, I surrendered. I had my own white-light experience. I said my first honest prayer: "I can't handle it; it's all yours." I didn't even know who to address my prayer to, but it didn't matter. After that, I said the Serenity Prayer and the 23rd Psalm over and over until I fell asleep. When I woke up, the craving to drink was gone.

The work was far from over, though, since being granted a reprieve from the compulsion to drink did not relieve me of the crippling character defects that led me to drink in the first place. It took me over a year to write my Fourth Step. I finally had to make an appointment to review my Fifth Step with my sponsor in order to complete the work. I was still writing as we sat down. It was hardly perfect, but it was tangible evidence of my willingness to move forward.

As we reviewed my work, my sponsor asked me to share the thing I was most ashamed of. I told him and he quietly said, "I did that too." It got easier from there. As I moved through the rest of my Fifth Step, I experienced the end of the terrible isolation that Bill described.

In the Sixth Step, a real shift happened, both in my life and in the discussion of the Step in the "Twelve and Twelve." From the terror and bewilderment in the first Steps, I began reaching out to become something better. I return to Steps Six and Seven over and over as my character defects, like weeds in a garden, sprout again. Over time, the worst excesses of my character defects have been removed, although the subtler forms are always waiting to reemerge.

Steps Eight and Nine mean more progress. I read that "a quiet, objective view will be our steadfast aim." As I made the list of those who I needed to make amends to, I relied on my sponsor and the experience of other group members for the encouragement to keep going. Over and over my sponsor reminded me it was just a list.

When I started Step Nine, most of the amends went well, although the person I hurt the most rejected my attempted amend, understandably so. I'd like to say I didn't falter in my steady and even purpose, but it took me a while to finish the Step. Today, my Ninth Step consists mainly of living amends.

I have found one of the benefits of working a thorough Ninth Step is fewer Tenth Step amends. "Restraint of tongue and pen" comes easier when I remember I'll only have to apologize later. Keeping the emotional balance found by working the first nine Steps is a daily task. Like everyone else, some days are better for me than others. What I find is that the emotional upsets aren't as serious or as long-lasting.

The permanent assets of the Tenth Step are amplified by the deeper connection to my Higher Power found in the Eleventh Step. Over and over through the "Twelve and Twelve," Bill breaks down huge concepts into bite-sized chunks. Calling meditation constructive imagination is one of the most important of those chunks for me. Sitting quietly in a chair, hiking, practicing Tai Chi and kayaking all allow me to make the connection to that Greater Reality. My Higher Power is always available to me—if I am willing to ask. The feeling of belonging that started with Step Five has grown into one of the linchpins of my sobriety and my life.

Finally at Step Twelve, I have moved from hopeless and dying to emotional sobriety and "the joy of good living." I have had a spiritual awakening from working the Steps. I perceive things differently now. When I'm restless, irritable and discontent, I have spiritual tools to use.

One reason I still attend AA meetings is because I love watching newcomers come in and seeing the miracle happen in them over time. I'm grateful to be a part of the miracle in any way I can. I can give someone a ride home. I can listen. I can share my experience if asked. I can also set up the room, make coffee and give out my phone number.

Once we finish the Twelfth Step in the book, that section is over. But my journey with the Steps continues. Just as we'll begin at Step One again and go through the book one more time, my sobriety and happiness depend on me working through the Steps again and again. It's a journey that I enjoy, as Spirit is always with me. My traveling companions at this Step study are truly precious to me, for there's always more to learn.

I understand why my grandfather kept going to his own "big book" study. If I'm given another 20 years, I'll still be attending this one.

Dwight H.
Pine Lake, Georgia

Rich Details
June 2013

After we purchased our 120-year-old house, there were many surprises in store for us. As we painted each room, we found that the hinges on the doors were handcrafted original brass and copper masterpieces full of rich details. However, they had been painted over numerous times, which made it impossible to see their original beauty. At some point a previous owner had decided that it would be easier just to paint over them than to remove, polish and replace them each time they renovated a room. Maybe they didn't feel the hinges were important enough to warrant all that work. Or maybe they decided that somehow they looked better painted. Either way, I am certain that the person who created the hinges never intended for them to look the way they looked now.

We removed the hinges from all the doors and discovered there was several coats of paint on them. We knew restoring the hinges to their original beauty would take some hard work. I had no idea how to go about this, so I spent some time doing research on the internet, until I found a site that seemed to have the answers. Then I went to work. First I boiled the hinges in vinegar, taking them out periodically to use a wire brush to dig the paint out of the detailing. I had to do this several times. Next I made a paste of lemon juice and baking soda. I brushed the solution onto the hinges, and then I gently polished away the tarnish with a soft cloth. This, too, I had to do several times.

I was amazed at the transformation that began to take place. The beautiful and intricate details of the hinges began to show through, and I saw the hinges in a whole new light. It took some hard work to get them looking like new, but I was proud to have brought them back to their original condition. I knew that to keep the hinges looking like this, I must periodically go back and go through the same process, but as long as I kept them polished and clean they would look this good for many years to come.

I am no different than those hinges, really. Alcoholism had obliterated all of the beautiful details that made me me. By spending my life trying to fit in and changing myself to feel accepted, I was slapping coats and coats of paint over my true self. Each new resentment I got was one more coat of paint I had put on. But then I found AA and it showed me how to go about scrubbing away all of the layers of resentment that had built up through my life, and then polishing what was uncovered. Steps Four and Five are like the vinegar and the wire brush, scraping away resentments one by one. Until those layers are removed, there is nothing to polish. By working the Steps, I am restoring myself to the condition in which God created me. Just as with the hinges, I may need to do the Steps several times before I am fully restored; and some routine maintenance will always be necessary.

If I get sloppy with my program, or try to do a "quick fix" by not working the Steps with rigorous honesty, it will be no different than throwing on another quick coat of paint. It may look OK in the short run, but eventually it will become lusterless and ugly. Just as I was willing to put the time and effort into restoring those hinges, I must remain willing to put the same amount of work into myself. This way I can keep my own rich detailing looking as the "artist" intended!

Mary O.
Lagrange, Illinois

STEP ONE

We admitted we were powerless over alcohol—that our lives had become unmanageable.

———————◆———————

The stories in this chapter speak to the devastation caused by alcoholism—loss of family, friends, careers. But liberation both from drinking and from the chaos of unmanageability is an extraordinary relief. There will be difficult moments ahead, AA beginners sense, but from Step One the bounty of sobriety springs. As Deborah G. writes in her story "There Will Be Blood," "That's when I embraced AA. My life had become unmanageable ... My last drink was August 11, 2010, and I don't miss it one bit. I never want to go back to that dark, ugly place." So many AA members look back at Step One and remember it as the joyous moment when their sobriety truly began.

Unmanageable, What's That?

January 2016

I began drinking when I was 15. Alcohol was fun and made me feel a part of the crowd. It removed my inhibitions and my feelings of inferiority. I had found the secret to my happiness and I loved it. After my first drinking experience, I began to drink whenever possible, always to get that initial elusive feeling. Sometimes I reached it, but then I always overshot the mark. But as the Big Books says, I always drank for the effect produced by alcohol.

When I was drinking, I never experienced problems. Oh, I had them—I just never experienced them. When I became restless, irritable, discontented, worried, sad or depressed, I knew just what to do. I'd grab a bottle of problem-remover and poof, no more problems. I used alcohol to manage my life and it worked quite well for a few years.

As with all of us, by the time I reached AA at age 38, alcohol no longer worked for me. Alcohol was certainly my master, so I had no problem with Step One, at least the first part of it. I admitted I was powerless over alcohol.

However, I couldn't see how my life was unmanageable. After all, I still had a lovely wife, two beautiful children, a nice home and two cars in the garage. I was doing well at work and continued to advance in my career. I thought that once I solved my pesky little alcohol problem, life would be perfect.

A friend of mine once said, "The disease (dis-ease) of alcoholism begins when we stop drinking." Man, was he ever right. All the problems I had ignored, all the feelings I had stuffed over the years, came back and hit me like a freight train. I had stopped drinking but I felt worse than I ever had in my life, which was totally out of control. Apparently, AA just didn't work, I thought.

But there was a part of the First Step I hadn't taken. It was the part after the dash. I had never admitted my life was unmanageable.

As I saw it, my life wasn't unmanageable because of alcohol. It was unmanageable because I had never learned to confront problems and feel feelings. Alcohol had been my solution, not my problem.

I always wondered why our cofounder, Bill W., separated Step One into two parts, using a dash. I thought that one idea referred to the other. That is, my life was unmanageable because I was powerless over alcohol. Bill had a wonderful command of the English language and wrote very precisely. I looked up the grammatical use of a dash and found this comment by the writer Lewis Thomas, M.D., who wrote: "The dash is a handy device, informal and essentially playful, telling you that you're about to take off on a different tack but still in some way connected with the present course."

I believe Bill was "taking off on a different tack" when he separated the Step. I am powerless over alcohol, is one thought, and, my life is unmanageable, is a second thought. The two are related but should be read as two thoughts.

Over the years, I have seen folks come into AA and things start to get better immediately. There are no more hangovers. They are sleeping through the night. They begin riding on the beautiful pink cloud. The problem is that after a few months, reality sets in and life doesn't feel so good any more. Life begins to get worse. We all know how to make things better. We drink and then go through the downward spiral again. We become convinced that AA doesn't work. I believe it's because we never took the entire First Step. At least that was my experience.

The Steps don't help us get control of our drinking. They help us get control of our thinking and our actions. Only half of Step One even refers to alcohol. Once alcohol is out of the picture, the real work begins. We realize how unmanageable our lives are without alcohol, our problem-solver. The Steps help us handle our sobriety. Therefore, my new life began after the dash, and my recovery continues to this day. Often life throws me a curve, but I know I have the tools to hit it head on. Problems don't stay now, they evaporate.

Ted K.
Columbus, Ohio

No Defense
January 2022

Being a binge drinker, it was not difficult for me to stop drinking for a week or even a month just to prove I could do it. I also knew if you wanted me not to drink for three weeks, on the 22nd day you owed me big time and you were going to pay up. But since I had little trouble not drinking for a given period of time, I was certain I was not an alcoholic.

Once, while on one of these mandated dry spells, I was invited to go to one of the most beautiful places on this earth: an open house at a liquor wholesale warehouse. I found myself there in the presence of more booze than I could imagine myself drinking in a lifetime, with a friendly face saying, "What would you like?" Since I wasn't drinking, I mustered all my strength, courage and fortitude and said, "No, thanks!" Then I tried to hurry out the door.

But there was that voice. In the back of my head I heard a small voice say, "This time will be different." I returned to the bar. Soon the words, "I've never tried that new Canadian, the one in the wooden box," came right out of my mouth.

I don't remember if I took the people who were there with me back to their cars or how I even got home that night. I vaguely remember putting an empty glass down on the kitchen counter at home just before I passed out on the living room floor.

About five hours later, as I was beginning to come to again, my girlfriend came to my home. She was extremely angry. I had promised to pick her up from work just about the time I was passing out on the floor. For some mysterious reason, she didn't think standing on the street corner downtown for several hours was very funny. I responded with my usual lack of tact, which didn't go well.

The next day, I pulled together all my humility and went to her apartment, expecting the usual punishment: a lot of yelling, scream-ing and maybe even some slapping. These things happened to me quite often as a drunk. I had come to expect these as the price I had to pay if I wanted to drink.

But this time it was different. She simply said, "I'm not going to yell or scream. In fact, I am not even going to say anything. I am just going to give you my Big Book and ask you to read it. Open it anywhere and just read something. See if there's anything in there that you can relate to." Then she sent me home.

Nobody had ever treated me like that before. They screamed at me, they beat me, they even sent me to jail. But nobody had done this to me.

I had to wait a couple of days for my eyes to clear up enough to read. When I could, I followed her instructions to the letter. I ran-domly opened her Big Book. I happened to land in chapter five—a very bad idea for an active alcoholic. I only read two paragraphs, but they scared me so badly that for the first time I was more afraid of a drink than I was afraid to live my life without alcohol.

That night I went to my very first ever closed AA meeting. My girl-friend handed me that Big Book on November 19, 1981. I have not had a single drop of alcohol since that day.

J.C.
Peculiar, Missouri

There Will Be Blood
January 2014

After attending only a few AA meetings, I felt like my story was boring. Maybe I didn't have a drinking problem: no tickets, no wrecks, no jail, no lost jobs, no wrecked marriages, no loss of family. I had only been drinking heavily for two years.

I'd gotten divorced after 22 years of marriage, and I survived the death of my son semi-sober. But when my job was eliminated after 28 years and I was forced to retire, that was the beginning of my downfall. To me, my life was over then. I was useless. My parents and my husband were all alcoholic, but, of course, I was not. I was just distraught, confused, bored and lonely.

However, one morning I woke up and somehow during the night the open dishwasher door had broken, and I had a big bruise on my side. A month or so later, an antique table broke during the night—and my big toe was broken! How did that happen? I must have been walking in my sleep. Then another morning the handle on the nightstand was broken, and I saw blood on the pillow. When I looked in the mirror, there was a four-inch gash in my forehead, and I could actually see my skull! When the doctor stitched it up, he asked me how I did it, and I said I tripped. Following that, I broke a playpen, a footstool, some dishes, a few plastic rails in the refrigerator and an antique washbowl and pitcher. Not long after that, I woke up and saw that the toilet lid was broken and my left arm was kind of dangling (I now have a plate in my arm and a horrible nine-inch scar). I went to rehab for two weeks after that.

But then came that morning when I woke up in the back seat of my car—in the garage. The back of my head was all sticky and there was blood on the doors, the seats and all over me. I thought I had locked myself in the car and couldn't get out. When I finally could move, I saw that the front door of the car was wide open. And there was blood on the floor of the garage.

I was taken to the hospital, where two doctors said I lost a lot of blood and had almost died. I went back to rehab and realized then that the first time I quit, my head told me to. The second time, my head and heart told me: quit drinking or die.

That's when I embraced AA. My life had become unmanageable. I now go to five meetings a week and love it. This AA works, it really does. My last drink was August 11, 2010, and I don't miss it one bit. I never want to go back to that dark, ugly place. The scars will be there always, as a reminder of my descent into insanity.

Deborah G.
Fort Wayne, Indiana

Weekend in Jail

January 2015

At the end of a 14-year binge, I was drinking around the clock to stave off withdrawal symptoms. I could barely walk due to shaking and didn't realize how close to death I was. The prospect of recovery and going through a detox process was something I'd never heard of. But when I got down on my knees and said, "God, I surrender," I found myself in a hospital bed within 24 hours. When God puts a miracle in motion, he promises to finish it, even if it comes slowly rather than quickly. Step One suddenly crushed my denial.

I was blessed in the most interesting ways during a year and a half of sobriety, but after that I decided I still needed to do some "research." So I picked up wine and vodka again. Deaths in the family, changes in medications, failed relationships and childhood issues are a few of the excuses I used to justify my actions. What followed were two years of drinking and frequent visits to detoxes and rehabs.

Conveniently forgetting what one drink would lead to, I kept falling prey to romancing the drink and doing the only thing I knew to cope: tumbling back into drinking, with days, weeks or even months of sobriety. I even entertained the thought that maybe I could be "a normal drinker," though I knew this was wishful thinking.

In early 2012, I drank while on probation for a previous DWI, which led to two weekends in a county jail and having to wear an alcohol-monitoring bracelet. I walked into jail desperately trying to control the outcome of each situation. I was finally beginning to see that I was trying to control everything and everyone in my life.

Step One came to life in a whole new way that first weekend and remains one of the most profound occurrences I've ever experienced. The jailers put me in solitary confinement, since I wasn't going to be there long. I'd been looking forward to meeting some of the other women in there, finding out about their struggles and sharing my story. Naively, I thought that God was about to put me in their lives and use me to teach them, instead of going into it with the attitude of wondering what he was about to teach me. I desperately longed to interact with someone, but for three nights and two days I experienced God.

Before I turned myself in that first weekend, I had prayed to God to reveal what Step One, and being powerless over my life, really meant. He answered that prayer in a gargantuan way, because I was now in solitary and all I could do was pray and read. I got to go to the jail library for one hour each day and take out as many books as I wanted. Thankfully, an entire section of inspirational books awaited me. I randomly started pulling titles of interest and finding chapters about powerlessness that caught my eye. When I got back to my cell I realized I had brought back 15 books with many of the chapters earmarked.

One of the first lessons that hit home was that in jail I couldn't charm my way into getting what I wanted. Although I genuinely treated the jailers with respect, I was no better than any other criminal there. Jail was exactly what I needed: a degrading and humbling experience—one I had zero influence over.

I had to wash my hair out with a preventive lice shampoo, strip down and put on stiff orange pants and shirt and slippers and do my time. A small square glass window through which the guards used to look in on me every 15 minutes was my only glimpse into the hallway where inmates did their chores. I had a metal cot with an inch-thick rubber mat and one wool blanket. The temperature was frigid, and the idea of using the open shower, or the cold stainless steel toilet that faced the window, or the sink with no mirror, did not appeal to me.

I'll never forget the sound of the thick metal door slamming shut and locking me in. Normally I would have loved having my own room and quiet time to read, but shivering under severe white lights in a room made of concrete—where my ears were hypersensitive to every tiny sound a person made—made me stir crazy.

Each second seemed to linger like a bad day. When I wasn't reading, I found myself praying. Ironically, something in my heart started thanking God for what I did have. My praises became heartfelt as I found myself grateful for the warm blanket, all the books at my disposal, my own room, my time with God, food, safety ... and my husband. Thanking God, and really meaning it, changed my whole outlook.

My sponsor had given me an assignment to write down all the ways in the past week I'd tried to manipulate the outcome of situations. When I started penciling things down I found that I had written an entire page in small print. What a control freak I'd been! I realized that in the past, when I hadn't gotten my way and wanted some immediate gratification to change the way I felt, I drank.

I began to see that I was responsible for all the consequences I faced, and that they were necessary so I could see how out of control my life was, not only when it came to alcohol, but in my need to selfishly get my way. I read the Bible and a bunch of recovery books. It was no coincidence that everything I read spoke to me about how I'd been trying to play God.

I couldn't believe the number of epiphanies I experienced behind those bars. It blew my mind. The First Step in AA took on a life of its own in my heart and mind: God was loving me through his discipline, walking me through the trials, enlightening me to my egotistical ways, healing and changing me.

Since then, I've been reading *Twelve Steps and Twelve Traditions* and the Big Book with my amazing sponsor, which has led to other unexpected "light bulb" moments. I believe God put this incredible woman in my life to help me see the harsh realities inside me that I avoided by drinking for 17 years. I'm constantly reminded that the more I think I know, the less I actually do.

When my heart surrendered to God and AA in August 2012, the Steps started working me instead of me trying to manipulate them. I came to the point where I didn't want to drink anymore. Living and applying Step One in every aspect of my life taught me several precious lessons: 1) This life is not about me. I'm not God, and when I get out of the way, he opens my blind eyes, ears and heart to his truths and reassures me of his promises. 2) If I got my way every time, I'd be missing out on growth opportunities and robbing others of their own lessons. I need to always remember to pray for his will. God isn't a genie in a bottle that I can rub and expect him to grant my wishes. And 3) Ultimately, the weaknesses that render me powerless make me dependent on my Higher Power, which allows me to have an intimate relationship with him, making me stronger in his strength.

That first weekend in jail translated into a divine intervention. I had a spiritual awakening that showed me—through his endless grace and mercy—how much he loves me. I've seen God answer prayers, and they're usually not the way I wanted them to be answered. If he'd answered them my way, I'd have missed out on the miracles that often came disguised as trials.

Melissa W.
Granbury, Texas

Help Wanted
January 2021

I had been fired from my job as a food service manager, unable to even remember what had brought about such a calamity. All I knew was that a blackout bender had been involved.

The enormity of such a blow to my career didn't sink in until I found out, through an employment agency, that I'd been blackballed in the industry. I learned that I had sent an employee out to purchase a half-gallon of whiskey. I had caused my entire crew of six to become so smashed that our customers had reported us to our superiors. The news spread like wildfire through the upper echelons of our industry, rendering me a laughingstock.

I wound up making sandwiches in a coffee shop, a position in which I was unskilled, competing with countermen half my age and twice as adept. As I bungled my way through each day, my alcoholic anxiety found me shaking badly, unable to concentrate. I was also recognized at the coffee shop by a coworker who I had once supervised. This person knew the details of my previous firing and gleefully spread the word in the coffee shop. Soon, I was again pink-slipped.

I was so shattered by the fact that I was unable to hold down the most basic of jobs in food service. I had been fired from more jobs than I cared to remember, every single one the result of drinking.

I was in fierce denial about my drinking. My apartment was in shambles, strewn with dirty clothes and broken glass. I was unkempt. I couldn't eat without first settling my stomach with a shot or two. I couldn't hold a pen to write. I was afraid to cross the street because my drinking left me unsteady. I didn't know the day, the date or the year, and would often get lost on the subway. And now that I had been fired again, I felt real fear and uncertainty about my inability to support myself. I had nowhere to turn and was hitting bottom, though I didn't know that at the time.

I can't remember the exact order of my thoughts on that fateful day that I was bounced from the coffee shop. I do remember it was snowing and that I picked up the pay phone receiver in the vestibule of the coffee shop and asked for the number of AA. I recall babbling into the phone, afraid and unsure of what to do next. I really have no idea how I knew to call AA.

The person who answered my call helped guide me into the rooms. He became my sponsor and held my hand while I made it over the hump. That was my First Step, my step toward a sober life. Today, 10 years into sobriety, I start each day by taking the First Step again because without it, the only step left for me is my last.

David B.
New York, New York

Surrender

January 2021

O n a snowy day in late December, I noticed a large bird walking among the trunks of the pine trees in the yard of my rural Wisconsin home. While I watched the bird, an AA friend arrived and excitedly identified it as a bald eagle with an injured wing. We watched the eagle struggle in the deep snow, exhausted from his attempts to fly. We called Patrick, a friend who is a certified raptor rehabilitator. Within five minutes, Patrick was on his way to help the injured bird.

As the three of us surrounded the eagle, he tried desperately to flap his way out of our tightening circle. His last great effort to escape was a panicked and ferocious display of talons and flapping wings. We finally were able to throw our blankets over him and he was safely contained. Patrick, his hands protected by thick leather gloves, slowly and gently untangled the eagle from the blankets and spoke to him in soft and soothing tones.

Surprised at how quickly the bird had calmed down and surrendered to the reality of his situation, I asked Patrick, "He seems so relaxed. Is the fight over already?"

"These birds seem to understand the help concept," Patrick replied while stroking the head of the alert but docile eagle. "Since he was in your yard, we'll call him Howard," Patrick added, looking up at me with a smile.

We put the eagle into a dog crate, covered the crate with a blanket and "Howard the eagle" and Patrick headed to the veterinarian's office.

My thoughts returned to Patrick's words, "They seem to understand the help concept." For years I had fought and resisted the help concept and refused to acknowledge or surrender to the reality of my alcoholism. When I arrived at my bottom and all avenues of escape had finally closed, I reluctantly entered the doors of AA. There, I found the help I so desperately needed in the power of a "we" program.

The "we" that helped Howard consisted of me, my AA friend, Patrick, the veterinarian and raptor rehabilitation volunteers and specialists. The "we" that's helping me recover from my alcoholism are the people at meetings, the Twelve Steps, a sponsor, sponsees, AA fellowship and a spiritual connection to a Higher Power.

In early May, the Raptor Rehabilitation Center reported that Howard was beginning to fly short distances in the flight cage and that he might soon be ready to reenter the world of eagles.

That June, Patrick opened the door of the dog crate and Howard stepped out of captivity into the sunshine of the release site. Turning to the large gathering of well-wishers, he tilted his eagle head back and made loud raspy clucks as if to say, "Thank you all for helping me recover."

After lingering for a few unsure moments, Howard lifted in the warm summer sky and flew effortlessly across the wide Wisconsin River into the freedom and happiness of his new life. Like Howard, I too am thankful for my new life.

Howard O.
Cambridge, Wisconsin

STEP TWO

Came to believe that a Power greater than ourselves
could restore us to sanity.

———————◆———————

F or alcoholics who may have had an uneasy relationship with
organized religion, Step Two can be difficult. As Judy E. writes
in "Many Powers Greater Than Me," "I struggled all my life
with the concept of God." But what she and other AAs grow to believe is that "a Higher Power just means I have a source outside
of myself that I can go to, depend on and trust more than I trust
myself. I need to acknowledge that I can't do this alone ..." Sometimes finding a Higher Power happens right away; other times
(but hopefully not) it takes a collision, as in Richard V.'s "I Found
My HP Under a Flatbed Truck." But as you'll see in these stories,
the moment when it does happen is an immensely rewarding one.

My Prayer Was Answered
February 2022

Like most of us, I knew I was in trouble with alcohol long before I came to AA. During the last two years of my drinking, I went back to church to pray my drinking away. I'd go to church and just pray about my drinking. Then I'd get home from church and I'd be drinking again. It just wasn't working.

I crashed and burned and finally took that longest walk of my life to the door of an AA meeting. When I got through the door, I found the people inside were praying and talking all this God stuff. I just wanted to run, but I stuck it out.

I would say out loud in meetings that, "God let me down. I went to church and was praying to stop drinking and now I'm stuck here in AA." Finally a guy cross-talked me and told me that my prayer had been answered because I had arrived at the place where I could stop drinking.

That hit me like a brick wall. His comment gave me hope that my prayer had indeed been answered and that I truly was somewhere where I could stop drinking. He was right. My prayer was answered.

About two years later I was at a Roundup in the mountains of Virginia. At a workshop after the AA speaker meeting, we were all asked to share about "When and how I came to believe."

As soon as that question was posed, I flashed back to that meeting in early sobriety when that guy told me my prayer had been answered. That was the moment I came to believe in a power greater than myself. Turns out the Second Step was working me before I even knew it was working me. That memory has sustained me and gives me hope and strength to stay sober to this day.

Charley C.
Arlington, Virginia

A Place in the Sun
February 2016

I n the course of my alcoholism, I spent years in therapy and hundreds of thousands of dollars on doctor visits and medications. I suffered an intense suicidal depression and was labeled bipolar.

The April before coming into AA, I planned to kill myself. One day after work, I went home to end my life. I had been planning to do it for years, considering various options and performing research on the best means of doing so. So when I went to bed that April night, I waited for the house to settle down so that I could take a lethal dose of pills. I wasn't thinking about a thing—not my wife or my child. I just lay there and waited. After all those years of planning, my life was crumbling around me, and the final solution to all of it was tucked away next to me in a bedside drawer. Amazingly, I did not fill my drink and take the pills. Instead, I passed out. I awoke the next day with something I'd never had: a willingness to change.

The next eight months were tumultuous. First I lost my job; then the state got involved in my life. I was forced to quit drinking. I was dry now, but not clean and sober. A funny thing happened on my way to sobriety however. Even with an active pill addiction, without alcohol my life started to change. Suddenly, my doctors didn't think I was bipolar. Over time, they took me off my last medication and I came into AA. I started a new job and life got better for my family.

One month into sobriety, while working Step Two with my sponsor, I took my family to San Diego for a vacation. The fact that I was alive to be there and had a job to pay for it was amazing. One afternoon, we went to a dolphin show. It was one of those beautiful San Diego days; the sun was shining and the air warm. We sat down in the grandstands and got ready for the show. Out came the dolphins and the performers, all set to music. The show was nice, but I saw very little of it. My eyes and my heart were watching my 2-year-old daughter.

She was so excited as she watched the show. Her face lit up with such intense joy; I'd never seen so much happiness on another person's face. I was enjoying the show through my daughter's eyes, when I was suddenly filled with intense gratitude and light for being alive to witness the moment. For the first time, I paused to ask myself, Why? Why was I alive in this moment?

I had come into the Fellowship of AA an atheist. I used to call myself an agnostic, because I always felt it was disrespectful to openly deny the existence of someone else's God. During my first month in AA, I stared at those Steps on the wall with great fear, wondering how I could ever get past the need to believe in a God of my understanding.

I thought about how my life had changed since that April night I was going to kill myself. I had stability at home now; I was free from suicidal depression and psychiatric medication, with the beginnings of real happiness I'd not known for 10 years. Why hadn't I done the easy thing that dark night and simply filled that glass and taken the pills? Even in my alcoholism, I was always a man of action. When I made plans, I acted on them. It was such a mystery that I hadn't taken those pills that night. But right there, on a sunny afternoon, while sitting in the stands with my daughter, I realized that such things do not happen by accident. The thought shook me to the core: A power greater than myself had reached into my life that lonely April night.

Tears began to stream down my face. For the first time in my life, I felt the presence of God. While working Step Two with my sponsor, I had wondered how I could ever come to believe a power greater than myself could restore me to sanity. I now realized he already had.

It turns out I found a God of my understanding through the light and eyes of my daughter.

Kevin F.
Vancouver, Washington

Chubby Gods, Skinny Gods
February 2017

When I first got sober, I seemed to be always sitting at a Second Step table. Everyone there had their God. They talked about him like he was a cherished friend. Or more like a magical genie that granted them sobriety every day. They talked about "finding" him. Did they mean in a God catalog? They didn't say.

One day I sat there and thought, Maybe I'll just skip this Step. That night I went to bed and said to myself, What am I going to do about this "God thing"?

The next day I sat at yet another Second Step table. Was everyone on the Second Step? This table had a few oldtimers and they swore up and down that they kept relapsing until they found God. I cringed, wondering how a relapse was going to fit into my highly scheduled life. When you're newly sober, there's no room in your schedule to use the bathroom some days. At the table, one person said the Second Step is the foundation of the rest of the Steps. Without a good foundation in a building, they said, it's sure to crumble. Without the Second Step, my house would disintegrate underneath me. I wasn't ready for that kind of wreckage. How would I find time to clean up?

Later that night I talked to my peers in the halfway house about their Gods. They all said they were not too worried about it. Soon after that, one of them relapsed and had to move out.

As I kept coming to the AA tables, I soon noticed who had a God and who didn't. Those without a God seemed to do OK but they would fight a lot and gossip. Others, I didn't see any more. Some would leave and come back with horror stories of going back out. I went home confused. I said to myself, What am I going to do about this "God thing"?

One day I was gifted a small amount of time to be by myself with nothing to do. Idle time is scary for a newly sober alcoholic. Thankfully, I had no money. So I went to the library where I saw a poster of a church in Italy. The church was ornately decorated. I knew there must have been a reason they put so much work into that building. Oh, that's right, God!

I looked up "religions" while I was at the library. I got out a stack of books, some of them with names I could not even pronounce. Gods of every size, shape and color. Some Gods had the iconic, skinny look of someone who needed medical attention. One God was chubby. One had a belly I could rub for good luck. There were male Gods, female Gods, cat Gods and dog Gods. There were planet Gods too, but I was too fair-skinned to worship the sun. When I was a child, I thought King Neptune was the God of swimming.

Back at the Second Step table again, someone said that God was everywhere. Could it be that simple? I seriously doubted whether God was at the crack house or those sleazy after-hours clubs I used to frequent.

I scanned the tables at my next meeting. I saw a man who looked like Neptune from the library books. He had Vietnam and Jesus patches all over his vest. I thought he must have all the God answers. As he spoke, at first he made a lot of sense. Then he started to quote verses out of the Bible in a "hell and damnation" tone of voice. Some got up to refresh their coffees as he spoke. I got the impression from this guy that his God was working for him. This man had 30 years of sobriety. I also gathered from the others that this man's God wasn't their God. He wasn't mine, either. Scripture written in some old-world language was not for me.

That night, as I lay awake in bed, I got the overwhelming urge to go out and get a drink. Not having any money, and being tired from my highly scheduled day, I white-knuckled my bed sheets and hoped the feeling would go away.

I woke up in the morning from a drinking dream that felt so real. As I washed my face, I realized I had not actually gone out to drink, I had only dreamed it. I knew I needed to get a God soon.

In group therapy at the house, we touched on the subject of God.

One cranky older woman refused to seek a God. She said this was her 15th rehab. A young girl with dreadlocks and a ladybug backpack chose a unicorn for her Higher Power, which was how people referred to their Gods. It says in the Big Book that we can call him that, which makes God seem like a new concept but not as "new age" as having a unicorn as a Higher Power.

I went to an open meeting to listen to a woman who had been a waitress in Detroit's Playboy club in the 1950s. It was hard to imagine her as a young beautiful girl, let alone a Playboy bunny. She told many stories of what she had done and seen during her drinking days. A lot was edited out, she told us. She said that she had trouble with the whole "God thing" until the oldtimers made it real simple. My interest was sparked. She spoke my language. They simply told her she was not God and no man was. God is a power greater than ourselves that can keep us sober.

I sort of understood all that. But I didn't understand where I could get acquainted with him. Was there a God meet-up? Would my God have a name? Would he be mad at me for all the stupid things I've done?

The former Playboy bunny said I should talk to God even if I didn't know him. Every day, she said, "Talk to him. Pour your heart out. He's the only one who really understands you. Eventually, you won't feel uncomfortable doing it. It will be second nature to reach out to God. In the beginning, we are all strangers. With time, friendship with God blossoms, as it does with every friendship."

That night in bed, I spoke uncomfortably to him about my day and our new relationship. I didn't know how this relationship would work, but I had faith in what people told me.

Now I've been sober four years. I am not uncomfortable at all talking to my God. It's second nature. Through the years, I've had hardships and cravings, but God has somehow helped me. I don't know how it works, but my faith in God is constant and communication with him is comforting.

Michelle B.
Hazel Park, Michigan

Many Powers Greater Than Me
February 2019

When I came into AA, I was a nonbeliever, or so I thought. I struggled all my life with the concept of God. I believe in the existence of God so I know I'm not an atheist. I know from my own experiences that the existence of God is knowable so I'm not agnostic either. I'm not sure what I am … and I'm not sure it really matters. But I knew I needed a Higher Power to work the Steps and stay sober.

I tried using the group as my Higher Power, but I found that I couldn't pray to my group. My sponsor wanted me to take certain actions, whether I believed in them or not, and one of those actions was praying. So I got on my knees every morning and asked something to help me stay sober and I thanked that something every night.

I learned over time, with the help of my sponsor, that I wasn't really a nonbeliever. I was just very angry with God because my daddy died when I was a little girl. I chose to stop believing in God because things just happened, there was no one to blame and no reasons to search for. It was easier not to believe.

My sponsor pointed out that I couldn't be angry at something that didn't exist. That was a light bulb moment and it opened my eyes and my mind to be willing to believe.

With some time and personal experience, that anger began to fade. As I stayed sober and life got better, I began to believe that that "something" I prayed to was God. I felt God much more in my head than in my heart.

It was suggested that I try to seek God in order to develop the sort of personal relationship I wanted with God and had heard other AA members talking about. I worked hard trying to do that. I looked for him in nature. I looked for him in those small coincidences, and I went to church for the first three years of my sobriety.

The God they talked about in church was different from the God I heard about in meetings. Church ended up provoking more questions than it provided answers. I had the belief, but very little, or no, faith. I still didn't know if God heard or answered my prayers. I didn't know what God did or didn't do. I didn't know what his part was and what part was mine. But I did know that God brought me to AA. I knew he wanted me to stay here and that he gave me the strength I needed to stay.

Even though I'm not sure he hears or answers my prayers, I keep praying. I keep taking the actions. I talk to him all day. I ask him for help. I bring him my fears and concerns and I ask him to give me strength. I even share my doubts with him. Just taking the actions without faith calms my fears, provides relief and brings some peace.

I know God loves me even though I may never be able to feel that in my heart. My lack of faith has kept me up at night wondering if what I do have is good enough to keep me sober. I learned I don't have to have all the answers, but I have found a way that works for me.

To me, depending on a Higher Power just means I have a source outside of myself that I can go to, depend on and trust more than I trust myself. I need to acknowledge that I can't do this alone, that I need help to stay sober and to make my life manageable. So, I pray to God.

I have a sponsor who I can see, hear and trust. I have friends to help me through the rough times and to share the good times. I need all of them to stay sober and they are all powers greater than me. I have five years of sobriety now so I know it works. And I believe it will continue to work one day at a time, as long as I know that I am not God and that I can't do this deal alone.

Judy E.
Orland Park, Illinois

Safe & Loved

July 2023

I had a great deal of difficulty getting past my Second Step to my Third. I was one of those who *Twelve Steps and Twelve Traditions* speaks of as people who sometimes have it worse than others connecting to AA, as "they have tried faith and found it wanting."

I had dedicated my life to the God I did not understand despite years of training in preparation for becoming a minister. I thought I understood God and could tell you how many angels could dance on the head of a pin. But that same God I thought I understood also hated me and condemned me to hell because not only was I an alcoholic and addict, but I was also gay. I tried for years to change all those things and to "pray the gay away," but nothing worked. I hated myself even more after I was suddenly dismissed from ministry training because they discovered my sexuality.

I felt like I lost everything, including the future I was working toward, and this rejection fueled my disease big time. I was now convinced that God, as I understood God, and a church of more than a billion people had exiled me because of who I was. So when I came to AA, I hit a huge roadblock. I couldn't believe in the God I had because it hated me so. Putting my will and my life in God's hands was not an option. I felt hopeless.

My sponsor at that time was a sympathetic man with a similar history of religious training. I was amazed that we had met and that our backgrounds were so similar. And he could see my despair.

"Perhaps we're trying to take this too much at face value," he said, suggesting we back up a bit. "Perhaps you could approach God a different way." He said my understanding of God clearly wasn't working for me and had left me broken. "Are you willing to say 'Thank you for sharing' to your well-meaning church folk and try something different?" he suggested. "Perhaps you need a new God of your understanding. What do you have to lose? You're already in exile."

I felt both great relief and great terror. With that statement, my sponsor had taken away the pain, guilt and shame I had been holding onto for years. But he had replaced that with utter terror by suggesting that I walk away from the faith of my youth and college years in which I had invested so much time and energy. What was I to do? He asked me to take a strange leap of faith—the principle behind Step Two—into what I thought was insane territory. What he said next blew my spiritual mind: "If you look back through your life, are there any exceptionally good people who have shown you care, love and attention, people who were probably much older than you, most likely dead?" he asked.

After a moment, I had a great feeling well up inside me in the image of my grandmother. She had passed on when I was 14. She was an avid church-goer and an elementary school teacher in our small town. She cared for me when my drunken mother was rampaging. She showed me great love and compassion. Everyone knew Grandma Emma—she had taught for 40 years—and almost anyone who knew her would say, "You're Mrs. B's grandson, aren't you?" Just being near her had made me feel safe, strong and loved. If there was a woman who would be in whatever heaven was, it was her. I told my sponsor, "Yes, my grandma. She is all of those."

"And could you talk to her about anything?" he asked. "Oh, certainly," I answered. "She wouldn't judge me, and she always gave me guidance. I wish she were still here." He then said, "Well, why don't you talk to her? Why not reach out to her? Maybe she can be your Higher Power for now."

I was dumbfounded. My sponsor was asking me to talk (or pray) to my grandma as a Higher Power. Was he crazy? And then he said something that hit me hard. "Your grandmother is good, old and dead. That spells G.O.D. to me. At the very least, you'll be able to turn your will and life over to Grandma, no?" I said, "Well, yeah. I could do that." Then he suggested, "You don't need to hold on to this belief forever, but long enough until you find a God of your understanding.

I've found it's helpful to ask the help of people who seem to know God, especially if they are closer to him now in the next life. If you can talk to her and not feel judged or hated and loved, it's at least a good start. Let her do the work for you."

So my grandmother served as my Higher Power for several months and I began to find other people who seemed to fit that G.O.D. criteria. Soon I had a small group of people who I was able to trust and pray to for support and guidance. It turns out that many older, strong people had watched out for me over the years of my mother's drinking, and they were helping me in my own struggles with recovery. I felt stupid praying to her, but I stayed sober.

Eventually things changed. I came to a larger understanding of a God who cared about me, not despite my being gay, but because I was a gay man in recovery. After I did my Fourth and Fifth Steps, I felt bigger and more and more trustworthy. I even began to see how some—not all—of my old seminary teaching seemed to be helpful and gave me a framework to talk about the change that was happening to me. I wasn't a person God hated. I was loved and, to this day, I simply say to my more evangelical or orthodox Christian folk: "I've already found my Higher Power and I'm quite happy. Thank you for sharing."

I'm thankful for my sponsor and my Higher Power for giving me a "backdoor" to a grander and more inclusive spirituality now. And I thank my grandma for opening it.

Christopher M.
Pompano Beach, Florida

Borrow Mine
January 2020

When I came into AA, I was spiritually bankrupt. Due to years of heavy drinking and a series of life experiences, I was depleted of any belief system. By the time I was 17, I had lost six people in my family to death: my father when I was 8, my sister when I was 9, my mother when I was 14, my grandfather and my stepgrandfather when I was 17. I also had a very close friend die when I was 17. As far as I could tell, I didn't think God was loving and on my side in life.

I got sober in 1985 at the Coral Room in Miami. They didn't care about my wonderful theory of evolution; they simply told me to get on my knees and pray. I had this AA friend named Jim with about three years sober, and the two of us would sit and debate the God thing. Now Jim was a scientist and we both had these wonderful theories on evolution. Oh, we had great ideas and thought the God thing was good for you AAers, but we were sure that we would have to find some other resource to keep us sober.

The oldtimers in the Coral Room told me that to stay sober, one simply had to find a Higher Power that one could do business with, and it could be the God of my own understanding—or AA itself. They said it's God who keeps us sober and the time might come when the only thing between me and the next drink is this Higher Power.

Fortunately for me, I chose a sponsor who didn't care what I believed in. She simply told me to get on my knees and pray. Which I did with a heart full of fear. Not so much a fear of drinking, but because I was afraid of her, and of not doing what she told me to do! I didn't know how to pray, but there I was, on my knees. So I started ..."God"... and then all I could think of was that I needed help, so I added, "Help." From that first scanty prayer, wonderful miracles began to happen in my broken life. And somewhere along the line, I came to believe that there really was a God, and a God personal to me who cared about me just like it describes in our Big Book.

Around that time, I became concerned about my friend Jim, as he did not have a Higher Power yet. The day I announced to him that, "I got it, I think I got the God thing!" he wished me well and the subject was dropped. Weeks later, still genuinely concerned that Jim might drink, I said, "Jim, maybe you could use my Higher Power until you find one of your own." I told him that I wasn't keeping my Higher

Power too busy and I was sure he wouldn't mind. Jim thanked me and we never spoke of the God thing again.

Sometime later, I moved away and wondered from time to time how my friend Jim was doing. A few years passed, and I came back to Miami to visit that meeting, and Jim was there. When it came Jim's turn to share, he said, "I had trouble finding a Higher Power my first three years sober, and a good friend loaned me her Higher Power. It works really well for me, and I have not found it necessary to find one of my own."

Wow! I had no idea that Jim had accepted my offer to loan him my Higher Power. He had never mentioned that to me. How interesting it was to learn that Jim was able to stay sober with a Higher Power he borrowed from me.

Since that day, I have tried as best as I can to not consume 100 percent of my Higher Power's time so my dear friend Jim can always borrow him.

If you're having a difficult time finding a Higher Power, look around your meeting room and see who seems to have a really good one. Perhaps they'll let you borrow theirs for a while.

M.L.
Placitas, New Mexico

I Found My HP Under a Flatbed Truck
February 2014

I sat upright in the middle of the street, noticing the clear Carolina blue sky and the stillness that surrounded me. I had just managed to lay down 600 pounds of rubber and steel in the form of a motorcycle, my bike skidding to a halt under the rear of the flatbed trailer. My right leg was pinned under the rear end of my bike and my right thumb rested in a position perpendicular to my wrist. I couldn't help but notice that I was extremely calm. It was as though time had stopped. I was acutely aware of everything around me and because of this, or maybe in spite of this, I knew that everything was going to be alright. Not just for today, but every day.

A year and two days earlier I had begun a journey into sobriety, but on this day, Sunday, Sept. 30, 2007, I was riding my motorcycle to a Twelfth Step meeting. When I left my house in Waxhaw, the sun was holding its mid-afternoon heat of 82 degrees, but it was sure to drop 20 by nightfall. Tossing my lightweight jacket into my saddle bag, I put on the leather instead. During the six months I had lived in this rural southern town, I'd learned a chill could hit when the road dropped into a hollow. The leather was sure to come in handy later that night. Little did I know how handy.

I rode about 10 miles along a route I had traveled many times before. I had just turned onto Potter Road, slowing to 35 to lean into a small turn approaching a hill. As I reached the top, I noticed a pickup truck ahead pulling a flatbed trailer filled with bales of pine needles. The flatbed was stacked high enough to obscure the truck's brake lights, and there did not seem to be any lights on the trailer. It took a moment for me to realize that the truck was at a dead stop. So with less than 100 feet ahead, all I could do was apply the brakes and hope for the best.

The year leading up to this moment had been a miracle year. I somehow had managed to stay sober by following suggestions and working the Steps. I never expected to be sober and living in North Carolina. It was only by the love and generosity of my sister and brother-in-law that I ended up here. Less than a year earlier I was living in New York City, trying to figure out how to pay rent and wondering if I'd ever get my life back together. Severe depression and an obsession with alcohol and other substances had kept me from attending to a job that paid six figures and offered a bright future. I was seeing a psychiatrist two and sometimes three times a week, and spent entirely too much time looking out my fourth-floor window wondering if I would die if I jumped. Then on September 28, 2006, I surrendered and began my journey.

I was told from very early on that reliance upon a Higher Power is necessary to stay sober. As I progressed in the program I wanted to understand my Higher Power, to come up with a working definition of my God. The more I searched and tried to connect with the God of my youth, the further away I drifted. I began to question the very existence of God. It was beginning to feel as though I was in crisis. Without God I would surely drink again; at least, that's what they told me.

And now here I was, heading fast into the back of a truck. The bike began to skid and the rear wheel fishtailed to the left. I began to go down, and in this moment I was filled with an overwhelming silence and peace. I didn't hear the tires screeching or metal scraping on the pavement; instead it was quiet, you might even say deadly silent. But I wasn't dead; in fact, I was alive. I sat up, doing my best with my left hand to remove my helmet and goggles, aware of the severe pain throbbing in my right hand. The realization of what had just happened filled me with a tremendous urge to pick the bike up and get out of the street.

But I wasn't going anywhere. My leg was pinned under the weight of the bike. Next I saw that my right thumb had been dislocated, forming a 90-degree angle with my arm. I popped it back into place.

State troopers were on the scene within minutes and then ambulances, sheriff's deputies and fire trucks. They asked if there was someone I could call to meet me at the hospital. I called my sponsor. After examining me, the EMTs strapped me to a board and blocked my head. They cancelled the helicopter (I may have missed my only chance to ride in a helicopter) and off we went to the hospital.

It turned out I only suffered road rash, a dislocated thumb, a separated shoulder, groin strain and a whole lot of aches and pains. It was amazing I wasn't hurt more severely. Perhaps it was a miracle, the hand of God reaching down to save me. I don't know, but something happened to me that day. Maybe it was nothing more than shock and an adrenaline rush, but that day, sitting there in the middle of the road, I was struck by an awareness of something greater than me. I discovered a peace, a serenity and an awareness I had never felt before. My life was changed—forever. For the first time in a long time, I knew I was going to be OK.

All my life I had always wanted to feel connected, to belong. I was looking for some great purpose and meaning, thinking that I had to achieve and succeed and live up to all of the expectations that had been set for me, when all I really wanted was to feel at peace, to be happy. I looked for happiness in relationships, things and money. I searched for peace in churches, gardens, museums and temples. I thought that somehow, if I had the right stuff or the right wife, the right job or the right car, I would finally attain the peace and happiness that had eluded me for so long.

Sitting there with my leg trapped under the bike, taking in the beauty of the fall day, the smells of grass, dirt and pine, the feel of the earth beneath me, I felt a sense of belonging. I belonged to everything. It would be wrong to say that I experienced happiness there in the street, but it was not far from joy.

That day I learned that peace and happiness are within me. They are not found in things; they can't be bought or given to me by someone else. I only need to stop and pay attention to access them.

I don't know if I found God in that wreck, but that's OK. I'm not sure it really matters. Today I have faith that I will be taken care of. I don't know by whom or how or why. I just know that I am part of something bigger, and when I am present, life is beautiful.

Richard V.
Charlotte, North Carolina

STEP THREE

Made a decision to turn our will and our lives over to
the care of God *as we understood Him.*

————————◆————————

T he well-crafted, personal tales in this chapter focus on a key
phrase in the history of AA. Bill's first draft of the Twelve Steps
talked a great deal about God, but when he showed it to fellow
AAs there were those who thought the echoes of explicitly Christian
doctrine would keep other faiths as well as nonbelievers away. The
phrase "God as we understood Him"—according to each individual's personal beliefs—became the compromise, Bill wrote, that "wid-
ened our gateway so that all who suffer might pass through." The
stories in this chapter capture pivotal moments when we "made a
decision" to allow our Higher Powers to take on those burdens we
cannot handle—and the freedom that ensues from our willingness
to surrender.

Handle With Care

March 2014

I firmly believe that it was in Step Three that I made the mistake that led to my "going out" in November of 2010, after five months of white-knuckled sobriety. My sponsor and I had begun my Fourth Step, but I apparently missed something in the previous one.

I had read the words in the Third Step a million times. I thought I fully understood the meanings of each word, but I had changed the meanings to fit my preconceived notions and prejudices.

I was at one of my meetings when I suddenly realized that the pivotal word in this Step is—care. So I looked it up. Foremost, the word has no shame to it. There is no control, servitude, or any other form of denigration, humiliation or degradation implied by that word. But I had chosen to infer that there was. I realize now that I was just unwilling.

I can't say that I've now gotten over all my prejudices—I clearly haven't. But what I can say is that Step Three doesn't have anything to do with them. It's more a declaration of my willingness to allow my Higher Power to take on the burdens I can't handle myself. To allow him into my life with the understanding that only he can do everything—I can't.

Step Three has a totally new meaning for me now. Where I once thought it was more of a sentence imposed on me, I now see it as a gift being given to me. I get to allow my creator to care for and protect me. All I have to do now is accept that gift. It's actually a chance of a lifetime. It's my chance to choose life over an alcoholic death.

Mark L.
Stagecoach, Nevada

Decision in the Desert

March 2022

t was 8:00 P.M. and I had just finished most of the post-flight routine after a 10-hour surveillance and reconnaissance mission while deployed somewhere out in the desert. Post-flight duties included turning off all my mission systems, cleaning and bagging up the trash, putting covers on the engines of the aircraft and gathering all my intelligence collected from the mission. I was tired to say the least.

All I wanted to do was jump in the duty van and ride back to our tents for some food and shut eye. But I was still a "nugget," an unqualified non-acoustic operator, that had to take out the ... well I won't say what it's called. Let's just say it was one of the awful duties handed off to the new "guys" like me.

What I had to empty was a slender four-foot-tall canister with a lid on the top. Yes, that is what we relieved ourselves into during flights as there wasn't a real toilet. I was hauling this awful bucket across the flight line to dump it into a real toilet, which was really a trailer holding a few portable toilets. As I was hauling it, I swung it too hard and it spilled 10 different aircrewmen's urine all down my leg, soaking my flight suit.

In my rage, I flung the container to the gravel just off the flight line and dumped it. After returning it to the airplane, I stomped to the flight gear tent. I was the last one of my crew to drop off my vest and gear. As I made my way to the smoke pit, I noticed none of my crew was anywhere in sight. They had left without me, leaving me to find my own way back to the tent compound. Luckily, there was another crew heading back and I jumped into the van with them, reeking of you know what.

I was dropped off at the common area. This common area consisted of a huge tent with tables, chairs and of course, a makeshift bar.

People were drinking, playing cards and socializing. Everyone was having a good time drinking, except me.

A fellow aircrew member came up to me, joyfully drunk, slurred something at me with his beer breath and bounced away. I was exhausted, angry, lonely and sober. All I knew was I didn't want to drink and yet his breath whispered sweet nothings into my mind, reminding me how easily I could blur out these emotions.

I walked back to my tent, showered and changed. I grabbed my Big Book and went to the smoke pit. While chain smoking with tears flowing down my cheeks, I began to say over and over in my head, I don't want to drink.

I prayed through sand-gritted teeth, asking my Higher Power to keep me sober. It was more like begging and pleading. I didn't want to go back to that horrid dark place I had just crawled out of not a year ago. I flipped to a page in the Big Book and started to read. Eventually I read, "Once more: The alcoholic at certain times has no effective mental defense against the first drink. Except in a few cases, neither he nor any other human being can provide such a defense. His defense must come from a Higher Power."

From the moment I read, "His defense must come from a Higher Power," I knew what I had to do. A feeling of calm and serenity flooded over me. No one was going to stop me if I wanted to drink. Knowing I was an alcoholic wouldn't stop me either because I had continued to drink in the face of negative consequences for years.

From the age of 15, when I had my first drink, I was a full-blown alcoholic. There was never a middle ground for me. The second that alcohol hit my stomach and warmed my insides, I knew I had arrived. Immediately, it quieted the obsession gnawing away at my gut because it was finally quenched.

With the thought of my Higher Power being my only defense out here in the endless desert, I closed my eyes and took a deep breath. I began to think of the first three Steps that I had done with a sponsor before I left. Until that moment in the desert, I had been giving lip service. I had the best intentions, but the work I was doing with another alcoholic just wasn't hitting home, until now.

First, I conceded to my innermost self that I was an alcoholic. I surrendered with everything inside my being. Second, I came to believe in a Higher Power because I could feel its presence all around me at that moment. All my fellow alcoholics' faith encompassed me, and I was in the middle. Third, I relinquished all power I thought I had and handed it over to that Power. I had no idea what that Power was, nor did I care, but I knew if I wanted to live I had to do it.

That was the first spiritual experience I'd had since I was a little girl who had forsaken God when terrible things happened in her life, and she didn't understand why or how this God had forgotten her. Now I was an adult who had made it through hell. I thought I had made it through entirely by myself, but now I realized that all along my Higher Power was there guiding me so I could make it to the other side alive.

I made it through that night without a drink with the help of a Power greater than myself. And all the other days after so far.

Dee Anne P.
Oak Harbor, Washington

Relax Your Grip
March 2018

A few years back, my wife and I were fortunate enough to find ourselves on a vacation together with my sponsor and his girlfriend in Hilton Head, South Carolina. Morning coffee and quiet times of prayer and meditation were often followed by 7:30 A.M. eye-opener meetings and the opportunity to meet other like-minded vacationers from the East Coast.

The chance to have this time together with my new sponsor, Dave, following the loss of my 20-year sponsor, John, was indeed providential. It gave each of us an unfettered period of time to talk and learn from one another how we apply AA's Steps to our thinking and living problems, as well as the chance to take stock of the myriad blessings in our recoveries.

One morning, Dave suggested that we take our bicycles and his two-handed kite to the beach. It was a sunny day and a moderate breeze created ripe conditions for kite flying. Until then, my experience with kite flying had been confined to the one-handed variety. As we set forth, I felt my pet character defect—contempt prior to investigation, fueled by pride and perfectionism—rear its ugly head.

To my consternation, Dave assembled the two-handed kite quickly. I really did not want to partake in this mundane and impractical activity on a day when we could have walked and profitably engaged in some profound sharing of our long-term recovery journeys.

After letting out about 75 feet of kite string, it became my task to lift the kite into the breeze as it blew onshore that bright morning in March. With seeming ease, Dave was able to keep the two-handed kite up in the wind after only two attempts. Another character imperfection of mine—jealousy—began to rise in that onshore breeze.

Now, it was my turn. Before he positioned himself to lift the kite for me, Dave made a simple suggestion to this "contempt prior to investigation" alcoholic.

"As I raise the kite into the wind," he suggested, "bring your elbows together and keep a loose grip on the kite handles. Let the wind carry the kite."

In my willful manner, I proceeded to do exactly the opposite of his suggestion. Hands clutching the kite handles and elbows apart, I tugged the kite strings, only to witness the kite come crashing to the sand at least a dozen times.

Each time the kite crashed, Dave would dutifully run after it, again gently lifting it, reminding me to relax my grip and let the wind carry it. I was discovering anew that my "lone courage and unaided will" could not raise the kite into the wind.

I then suggested that perhaps this was not going to be the day for me to fly this particular kite. Dave suggested that I give it one more try. As I half-heartedly took the kite handles, Dave raised the kite again.

But this time I knew that somebody or something else had entered the moment. As I relaxed my grip and brought my elbows together, the kite began to ascend into the wind. My previous contempt was suddenly replaced by a childlike spirit and confidence that my Higher Power was now handling this heretofore impossible task. The kite remained airborne for almost 20 minutes.

In fact, my sponsor, his girlfriend and my wife needed to tell me that it was time to bring it down as they were preparing to leave the beach.

Last year my wife was diagnosed with cancer and we entered upon an extended period of anxiety, fear and uncertainty as we made the rounds of doctors to identify the cancer and lay out a course of treatment. As treatment began, we found ourselves getting into the car one subfreezing morning to go to radiation therapy.

As I slid behind the wheel, I glanced over at my wife, who displayed the fear and worry we were both feeling. I started the car and tightly gripped the wheel. As I did, my thoughts raced uncontrollably. Then, a simple idea entered my consciousness. I remembered the words of my sponsor from that day on the beach: "Relax your grip and bring your elbows together." As I recalled that moment, I began to "comprehend the word serenity." I somehow knew that I would come to know peace during the difficult period ahead.

Through the grace of God, the care of wonderful medical staff and the support and prayers of family and AA (my sponsor heading the list), my wife's cancer is today in remission. From that March day on the beach, I learned that many of my thinking and living problems have their genesis in the "misuse of willpower."

When I try to bombard my problems—and sometimes hidden opportunities—with my self-will, the only thing I can expect to experience is frustration, disappointment, and later, remorse over missed opportunities my Higher Power has in store for me.

Bringing my will into agreement with God's intention for me today enables me to again comprehend the word serenity and know peace. I am gradually learning that spiritual growth is, indeed, increasingly possible if I try, to the best of my ability, to practice these principles in all my affairs. And Step Three, along with a loving, patient sponsor and a two-handed kite, opens the door.

Paul M.
Valatie, New York

White Knuckles, Clear Eyes
March 2014

To celebrate my 15th birthday, my dad bought a couple of cases of beer and we had a party in our basement. It was a lot of fun. My friends and I drank and played pool all night. All of my insecurities and feelings of not fitting in disappeared with the first beer. Sometime in the early morning I remember staring at the can of beer in my hand and telling my friends that this was the life. One of my friends grew really angry and argued with me because his father was an alcoholic.

It was a moment of clarity, perhaps a warning from my Higher Power, but I just ignored it. That was October 9, 1965. The next 15 years were laid out for me: I became a daily drinker. From the beginning, I suffered horrendous hangovers and remorse, yet I kept telling myself it was always going to be different the next time. For many years, I tried to find that first glow again, but never did.

Flash forward to December 24, 1980. I was sitting with my first beer of the day and telling myself that I deserved to get drunk one more time. It didn't matter that I would get horribly ill. I deserved the pleasure. A case of beer had been in the fridge for three weeks while I was detoxing from all the pills I had taken for seizures due to a recent stint of controlled drinking. I had been found out when I finally told a shrink the truth about my drinking. The doc didn't want to deal with me then, and had set up an intake appointment with the rehab folks the first week in January. But that day I felt I deserved one more drunk. After two drinks out of that bottle in my hand, I had a realization that this would never work again. So I sat there in the darkness of my mind and soul—lost. I believe I then experienced my second moment of clarity: I poured the rest of the bottle down the drain. Then I became very angry.

The doctor had told me that unless I changed my attitude I would not be accepted into their program, as it would be a total waste of time. She stated that I either had to quit drinking or die. Her nurse gave me a Big Book, which led me to an AA meeting on January 11.

A little more than a year later, I found myself at the U.S. Navy's drug and alcohol counselor school. The sign over the door read, "The Best of the Best"—that certainly was not me. I had been having continuous drunk dreams since putting down the booze, really unpleasant dreams from which I would wake up covered in sweat and having to ask my wife if I had really drunk again. It was a hard year and a half of just not drinking, and all because I would not take Step Three. My sponsor had even backed me up against a Quonset hut and threatened to kick my butt if I did not begin to pray. He often would come to my house with his sponsor to pray with me, but I did not surrender. The only God known to me was a punishing God. I felt he had taken my and my wife's first child in 1977 as punishment for my actions.

About three weeks into school I had to go see the director. The drunk dreams had intensified as had the anger and fear, and I was not doing well in the program. When I reported to his office he told me to go hang on his door and not to let go until he told me I could. I would show him— I hung there, telling myself I could do this. A few minutes later, knuckles white and hurting, I fell off. It was then that I had my third moment of clarity. He did not have to say a word; the message hit me like a brick. I could not do this alone. And if I continued to attempt this I was going to drink again.

That very night in a trailer in San Diego, I took the Third Step with an AA buddy. Later that same night I had another drunk dream. I was in my usual bar, however someone came in before I took a drink and we left the bar together—sober. The next day, I packed my bags and went over to the treatment side of the house to work on some of those guilt and anger issues.

As a result of my third moment of clarity, I now have a loving God who's always with me. He lets me make mistakes, but he's always there when I reach out to him for help. Perhaps equally as important is that I know I've got to stay sober or lose everything. After I took the Third Step, the compulsion to drink lifted and I was able to redo Steps Four and Five and gain freedom from the past. Then I was able to move on and complete the rest of the Steps in order, instead of just Steps One and Twelve.

Today is my 30th anniversary of sobriety in AA. My life is filled with wonderful blessings. My Higher Power and the Fellowship taught me how to grow up, think of others and be of service. When I got here I just wanted to get out of trouble and not drink again, which has happened. The rest is just gravy on top of the roast beef.

Bill F.

Anaheim, California

Whole Lot of Ready

March 2013

Last Thursday, when I was diagnosed with melanoma cancer, my immediate thoughts went to acceptance and the Third Step Prayer. How in the world does that happen to someone who, just two years and 10 months ago, used alcohol as the answer to everything?

Each meeting I'd attended had somehow been exactly what was needed. It started with my Wednesday 7 A.M. meeting, when a fellow Irishman received his 33-year medallion. We were on the Sixth Step, and after we read, "Were entirely ready to have God remove all these defects of character," my friend added, "And that's a whole lot of ready!"

This has always been a checkpoint for me, usually finding I'm not a whole lot of ready and need to step back and see what's happening.

Well, that day I was a whole lot of ready and really felt at peace.

That evening, at my home group meeting, two other friends received 33-year medallions and we were on the Third Step. This has been my cornerstone, and I found myself thinking of the Third Step prayer, specifically the parts, "Relieve me of the bondage of self ..." and "... that victory over them may bear witness to those that I would help of thy power ..." I envisioned myself being held "in the hollow of his hand," which comes from an Irish proverb.

Thursday, I got the biopsy results. I arrived home feeling numb and at peace, and told my wife and son. I attended my 8 P.M. meeting and sure enough, a friend who's better at detecting people being sad than my old black lab came over and sat by me. As we broke into small groups, I told him the news. He said he would pray for me. As I shared my news with the group, I found myself thanking God for this program, for it had readied me for this day. I was in God's hands and I couldn't forget it. I needed to let go and let God.

Friday was weird. All the things I thought were important suddenly meant very little. I decided to take the afternoon off and contacted one of my AA buddies, asking him to meet me at a 7:30 P.M. meeting. Our trusted servant chose "anger" for a topic, but instead I talked about acceptance. It was now clear that the things which used to anger me weren't even worth thinking about. I was starting to comprehend the word serenity and know true peace. At my Monday 6 P.M. meeting, I listened closely as two newcomers shared their stories, remembering the support I received from my new friends during those first few days and weeks.

I'm convinced that God didn't help me beat my alcoholism to strike me down with cancer. I'm still a work in progress and have every intention of living long enough so I can say I'm sober longer than I wasn't. I have sentinel lymph node biopsy surgery scheduled for early next week. Afterward, regardless of the outcome, I plan to continue sharing my experience, strength and hope with others.

Tim P.
St. Paul, Minnesota

STEP FOUR

Made a searching and fearless moral inventory of ourselves.

———— ♦ ————

One primary reason for drinking is resentment—so often, each successive drink comes with the name of a person who has done us real or imagined harm attached. Writing a Fourth Step inventory list brings such resentments into the light of day and helps us understand, as Alex M. discusses in "Popping Up Everywhere," "... how much easier it was to play the victim and blame others for my messed up life rather than be accountable for my own role." Whether it's something as minor as a casual opinion voiced at a party (see Kiko M.'s "Turning Down the Volume") or the stark anger of a man who finds himself in jail ("That Sneaky Devil," by Robert C.), the Fourth Step helps us tamp down our egos, be better friends, spouses, partners and colleagues and live happier sober lives.

Dive In, the Water's Fine

April 2014

When I got to AA in October 1996, I was done. I'd been working in rock bands and in New York City nightclubs for years, and now I was hiding bottles and drinking room-temperature vodka all day to manage the shakes. I couldn't tell my closest friends, and the loneliness had gotten unbearable. By the time I made it to the rooms, I was ready to do just about anything anyone said.

I wandered in and out of meetings for a while anonymously, which is easy to do in Manhattan. But one day, for some reason, I walked up to a friendly guy who made the sponsorship announcement. I sputtered, "I need one of those," so he promptly took me over to a total stranger named Scott, who said he'd be my sponsor. To this day I still can't believe I went up to those guys.

Scott was a sweet, quiet Wall Street man, nothing like me. After the meeting he took me to a diner near Union Square and told me how he used to pace back and forth in front of the liquor store there at 8 A.M., shaking and desperate for it to open. I was sold. This guy knew what I was going through. That night Scott started taking me to his favorite meetings, and he hooked me in with other AA guys. I'll never forget him for that.

After a few months I began hearing people talk about doing Fourth Steps, and boy I was ready to roll up my sleeves and do mine. But Scott slowed me down. I think he wanted to make sure I had a Higher Power. After all, it says fearless inventory, right?

When it came time, I made columns just like the "Mr. Brown" ones in the Big Book. The resentments were the easy part. I had no problem listing those. However, when I went to write down what my friends, like Russ and Paul and Judy did to me, I couldn't figure out what to write, because they hadn't done anything to me! I realized then that

I'd been going through life expecting people to behave a certain way, and when they didn't, I would become resentful. What a revelation.

When I got to the "my part" column, I was even more stumped. I thought, What do you mean my part? I was a nice guy! I just couldn't stop drinking vodka all day. But when I asked myself if I could have been a better brother or son or friend, then a door swung open and I really started writing.

About three quarters of the way through, I began to bog down. That's when I heard this woman, Gerry, who used to sit and knit at my lunch Step meeting, say, "It's just a list. Write it down. It's just a list." That helped me, because I was trying to put down my whole life story and I was getting hung up on it being perfect. She also taught me that we do Step Four as thoroughly as we can, and I could always do another Fourth Step down the road. Wow, that helped me relax some. Nice. I also heard people say, "Look back but don't stare" and to keep moving. I could ask my sponsor for help. It was important to not get stuck. It's not about perfection.

I can't believe how much the Fourth Step has changed my life. I'm not the same guy as the guy I was before I did this incredible Step. I now know how I tick and how I have behaved. This Step helped identify my character defects, which led me to Steps Six and Seven, which then led me to my loving Higher Power.

One of the great gifts AA has given me is the ability to be there for others. Today I get to help a sponsee through his first Fourth Step, to assure him when he's frightened that everything is going to be OK. I tell him that the Fourth Step is our friend. It's not punishment. It's not an excuse to beat ourselves up. We did enough of that when we were out there drinking ourselves to death.

When I was a newcomer, I remember going to Step meetings and being amazed hearing people share about the relief they got from doing their Fourth and Fifth Steps. It reminded me of myself as a kid, standing on the end of the diving board, full of fear, while my friends were already splashing and playing in the pool, yelling "C'mon in! Jump!"

So pick up the pen. Dive in. It's cold at first, but believe me, the water's really fine.

Danny S.
Georgia

Popping Up Everywhere
April 2019

I n reading Step Four, I realized my main character defects were already listed: selfishness, dishonesty, resentment and fear. Resentment, per my grudge list, was easy to recognize. Dishonesty was also easy, since I lied about everything so you wouldn't discover my secrets. Fear was a defect because it was about losing something I had or not getting something I wanted.

These three defects boiled down to selfishness and self-centeredness. These got me into trouble in so many ways, especially when I believed I was all-powerful and could control every aspect of my life.

Writing my moral inventory of what I had done wrong in my past was a liberating experience. For once, I could be honest with myself and didn't have to keep those skeletons in my closet any more. They were like zombies. They wouldn't stay dead and kept popping up where they weren't wanted. When they did, I was flooded with shame and guilt. The committee in my head got fired up. Fear set in about what I did yesterday while in a blackout and what might happen tomorrow after all was discovered.

So I did Step Four exactly as it's suggested in the book, with a lot of help from my sponsor. I wrote about how I resented my parents, wife, family, boss, coworkers, neighbors, people from my childhood and some who had died long ago. I wrote about the injustices I had so stoically endured and all of my justified anger. I wrote about my fear of dying a long, slow, painful death from cancer and my fear of going broke and fear of people hating me ... and my fear of never being loved.

I wrote about my inability to have any kind of healthy or fulfilling relationship with anyone and why that was. I wrote about people I had harmed more than they had harmed me and some who hadn't harmed me at all.

I listed character defects I had never acknowledged or accepted as mine. As I saw it, those defects had always been someone else's. I wrote about how much easier it was to play the victim and blame others for my messed up life rather than be accountable for my own role in my miserable life.

At the end, I couldn't believe the mountain of manure I had created. It reeked. And it was all mine. I hadn't cleaned house, I had cleaned out my insides.

The book says, "When we decide who is to hear our story, we waste no time." No problem there. I wanted that pile of muck gone. So I did Step Five right away. It was long and a little scary, but it was such a relief. I could finally let go of the guilt and shame from my past, and see that maybe, just maybe, I could actually start a new life.

Alex M.
Louisville, Kentucky

A Sketchy Fourth Step
April 2015

'm an alcoholic, and I'm severely dyslexic. In school I got Ds and Fs. I was able to join the military because a friend helped me pass the test. I took a job in the service that did not require reading. Later, under a federal program I was able to take college classes. In college I needed to have someone read the tests to me out loud. I also had to give my answers verbally, instead of writing them down.

I'm now in my 50s and getting As and Bs in my classes. I hope that my story gives hope to newcomers and reminds them that there is a new way to live and that you're never alone. There are people in AA who can guide you through the Steps and help you see how they relate to your life.

My journey in sobriety began in the summer of 1980. I started coming to AA because my mother paid me to take my brother to meetings. I agreed because it covered my gas and gave me a little extra drinking money. I didn't consider myself an alcoholic at that time, even though on three occasions I was sent home because I showed up to work intoxicated.

I remember someone in a meeting suggesting to the newcomers to try not to drink for 90 days. I thought 90 days wouldn't be a problem, since I wasn't an alcoholic. So I challenged myself to two years, and just about made it.

During this first period of sobriety, I got a sponsor with whom I shared some personal things. One day, when I arrived early at a meeting, I thought I overheard her talking about me to another member. That's when I decided I didn't need a sponsor and I could do it on my own. I must mention that years later I came to realize that my first sponsor probably was not talking about me.

While sponsoring myself, I went through some very difficult times, including the loss of my father. In December of 1980, he committed suicide. I was the last one to talk to him. He sounded good and we talked about things he was doing at work and plans he had. About 30 minutes after our conversation, he killed himself. I believe he was in a blackout and didn't know what he was doing. I managed to somehow stay sober during this time.

In June of 1982, I went out and had a shot of whiskey and smoked half a joint. This was the last time I drank alcohol or used drugs. I realized that I was going to be out on the street and would have to sell myself to support my habit. I was not about to do this, but I was afraid to go to a meeting in my central coast area of California. And I was avoiding the AA hotline because of a woman I knew who worked there. She had given me rides to meetings and I had overheard her husband say that I would never get sober. So I couldn't call to tell her about my slip and prove her husband correct. Instead, I confided to my supervisor about my slip. He told me to keep it to myself and no one would ever know. But I knew. I kept thinking about what our sobriety chips say: "To thine own self be true." I realized at that point that I had to do something different. The truth is I was afraid that—like my father—I would commit suicide.

I went back to Stockton and called the man who became my sponsor until his death in 2007. He was my brother's sponsor. I liked that he knew my history through my brother. He required that every week I attend a Big Book study group, a "Twelve and Twelve" meeting, a women's meeting, an *As Bill Sees It* meeting, a topic meeting and a meeting with him. So I was at a meeting just about every day. I felt confident that everything I told him would remain confidential. I did as he and other AA members suggested, staying as close to the center of the pack as possible. It was very difficult to reach out to others and confide in others in the beginning and still is, but the fear is much less than it once was.

When we met, my sponsor and I started working Steps One, Two and Three. At this time I did not have a Higher Power. In the beginning, AA meetings were my spirituality. Today, I can say that I have a creator, but the term God still makes me cringe. I now have a Higher Power that I confide in every morning, and when I hear the term God, I tell myself that "G" stands for good, "O" for orderly, and "D" for direction.

When it came time to take Step Four, I told my sponsor I could not do it because I wouldn't be able to write it down. He told me to draw pictures of the things and events in my life that harmed me. About a week and a half later I came to him with a picture book I had created. We sat down and I explained every picture to him. Using the information I gave him and the things we discussed, we were able to complete all the parts of the Fourth Step. By the end, I had a list of my character defects and a list of people I needed to make amends to. I was able to complete the Steps with the guidance of this sponsor. I continue to work the Steps, but will always remember those early days with that sponsor. I appreciate how he was able to guide me through the Fourth Step in a way that suited my learning disability.

I found a whole new way of life after working the Steps. I hope that by reading this other members will see that there's more than one way to work the Steps—as long as we're willing, open and honest.

Wave P.
Fresno, California

Grandpa's Journal
April 2020

Above the bar in my parents' house hangs a photo of the USS West Virginia, a warship that was rebuilt after World War II. The photo is black and white and was taken long before my father was even born. In the picture, the third person to the left on the second row is my grandfather. It was taken when he was a young, handsome midshipman standing proudly in front of the ship. To the left of the photo, sitting on the bar, is a picture of him during his Navy days.

Relatives and friends who knew my grandfather say we look and act the same, that I carry a lot of the traits he did when he was alive. My grandfather died only a couple of months after my father was born so he never knew my grandfather.

Growing up, I would ask about my grandfather and they would say he died from a disease a long time ago. I always assumed he just got sick with cancer or something. That's what my family led me to believe.

When I came into AA, I was curious about a lot of things, including the history of the program, the nature of the disease and whether it is hereditary. As I sat at my father's custom-made bar one cold, wintery afternoon in mid-December, I asked my dad if he ever questioned that he might be alcoholic or if he was an alcoholic. "No," he replied, "but your grandfather was."

He went on to explain that my grandfather was just as much of a drunk as I was, if not worse, and that his cause of death was alcoholism. I asked if there were any more photos of my grandfather that might be accessible. My dad set his glass of Scotch down on the bar, went into his office and came back out with a box. In that box were some of my grandfather's items from nearly seven decades earlier.

There was a baseball signed by the 1923 Yankees, love notes to my grandmother, newspaper clippings, his dog tags and an old pocket-knife.

At the bottom of the box was a journal tied to a worn-looking book by some string. My heart stopped as I gently picked up that old weath-ered book. It was his Big Book and it was a first edition!

I placed his Big Book on the bar and proceeded to read my grandfa-ther's journal. The first pages described in horrifying detail the struggle, sadness, hopelessness and fear that grips one who is a subject of "King Alcohol." What my grandfather had documented was a description of exactly how I had felt prior to finding my way to AA.

I asked my father whether he had ever read the journal. He said he had but he became confused after reading the first few pages. He guided me to the sixth page. He pointed to some words and said, "This makes no sense. All that is written down are people my dad hated, I guess."

I about fell off the barstool, and for once not because of too many cocktails. I snatched the journal from his hands and felt a presence come over me—something almost supernatural. Those first pages of the journal were my grandfather's Fourth Step inventory. He de-scribed the war and, based on the entry dates in his journal, he ap-pears to have written this while he was stationed at Pearl Harbor.

Although I never knew my grandfather, we are linked together for-ever because we share the very same problem.

There was not much more in his journal after those pages. The booze caught up with him, I suppose. I still do not know for sure if the disease is passed down from generation to generation, but I do know that my grandfather, through ways I cannot explain, is walking hand in hand with me as I trudge this road of happy destiny.

Kyle F.
San Antonio, Texas

Gotta Write It Down

April 2019

Our book *Alcoholics Anonymous* gets right to the point when it comes to Step Four. The words "searching and fearless" are not to be taken lightly.

At first glance, our inventory process appears to be a simple procedure. Make a list, dealing with resentments first, since they are classified as the "number one" offender.

When I approached Step Four, I told my sponsor Ray (in a subtle effort to evade the issue entirely) that I was troubled by the Eighth Step. I could not get the list of people I had harmed started. But Ray just said, "Where is your list?"

"What list are you talking about?" I asked. "You know, the list you made in Step Four—the people you resent," he answered. "Oh, that list," I said. "I don't have it with me." "Well, go get it!" he said.

"I don't have it written down," I explained. "But I have a list in my mind." Ray gave me a look. "No good," he said. Then he opened the Big Book and pointed to the chart in the chapter "How It Works" which lists: "I'm Resentful At," "The Cause," and "Affects My." He gave me a piece of paper and a pen and told me to go into the den and make a similar list.

There are times in one's life when pointed and explicit direction are necessary to overcome real or imagined obstacles. Ray had the knowledge and understanding to help me deal with the imaginary pitfalls of Step Four in a manner that removed the objections I had.

We went over my list and added the all-important fourth column— my part in these resentments. Finishing with a fear and sex inventory, I was free to continue on with the process of cleaning up my past.

It worked then. It continues to work today. Ray's words come back to me often. Half measures do indeed avail me nothing. I found that a searching and fearless moral inventory is indeed the key ingredient in comfortable sobriety.

Terry E.
Elephant Butte, New Mexico

That Sneaky Devil
April 2016

After 22 years of trying to put my life together, and 1,237 days of sobriety, I found myself in a 6 by 12 cell, angry at the world and accused of harassment by the woman I loved for 17 years. I was so full of anger and revenge. I kept asking myself, How could this have happened?

Later that day, I saw a literature display there at the jail. It was filled with information on substance abuse, violence counseling, zootherapy (whatever that is) and job-related courses. None of these seemed to apply to me. I have a good job that I love, my boss is appreciative of my work, and I had quit hard drugs over 20 years ago with relative ease (especially when compared to my 10-year battle with alcohol). I had even spent three years in violence counseling that yielded results past my expectations.

Then all of a sudden, I saw in the lower right corner of the display rack two issues of Grapevine. I grabbed the June 2014 issue and shot through it. I felt somewhat better, calmer for sure, but something was still amiss. So I grabbed the May 2014 issue and started to read. As I neared the end of the magazine, I found exactly what I needed to hear. It was masterfully woven into Annemarie's story, "Note to Boss," about Warranty Five. It seemed as though she was talking straight at me. I felt the sting of anger mixed in with humility. I could almost see my grandmother's forefinger swaying back and forth. It was overwhelming. I wanted—needed—my Big Book, but it was back at home on my nightstand. So I turned to the back page and read the Twelve Steps. I promptly froze on Step Four. I immediately knew I needed to do an inventory.

I found a pen, and after putting just three items to paper, I was floored. I saw my self-centeredness and my impatience. I was still blaming others for my woes. I sat in my cell and bounced all of this off the wall for a while. I thought of what my sponsor Dimitri and my AA friend Diane would say. It became clear to me that my self-centeredness was definitely the issue, as the other two, impatience and blame, always brought me back to that. I always got impatient with people who did not cater to my self-centeredness (nearly everyone), and then I'd blame them for my reactions.

Suddenly I felt calm. I choked up a bit but continued writing ... so I could remember, I told myself. Then it hit me like a bus. I got a big smile on my face. My self-centeredness was in play again ... sneaky devil. This was not my idea. Was it not Annemarie's story that made me see the light?

As I sat there in my cell writing this account, my eyes filled with tears again. Maybe this could light the way for another poor soul seeking an elusive answer in the darkness.

Robert C.
Montreal, Quebec

Turning Down the Volume
April 2022

Recently I had the opportunity to DJ at an AA conference. To prepare, I put in months of work, attempting to absolutely perfect the list of music I would play. I was so nervous and full of fear about whether the people at the event would enjoy my music. My ego wanted my fellow AA members to think I was the best DJ to ever grace an AA dance. Needless to say, God had other plans.

The very morning after the fairly seamless and fun dance at the conference, I overheard an attendee make a comment about how bad the music was. I was shocked. After I put in months of hard work and musical preparation, how could someone say that my music wasn't any good?

As my body shook with rage, I turned to him and snapped, "Well, I was the DJ, you know." He looked at me and said again, "Yeah? Well, the music was trash."

I stomped off, my face flushed and my head swimming with resentment. Who did he think he was? For the next few hours, I spent time stewing with this resentment in my hotel room.

After a while, I went back to the conference. I ran into a newfound friend, Tim, while preparing for another portion of the conference entertainment and explained to him why I was so angry and hurt. "Isn't it funny," he said, "how you had a lot of people dancing last night and all you can focus on is this one guy's bad opinion?"

Then it hit me. Not only had I been so ego-driven in hoping to be showered by all with compliments about my playing, but I had also failed to realize that everyone's entitled to their own opinions. I can't please everyone.

Even in sobriety, I've always been concerned with what others think of me. I felt that if others approved of me, it would fill the God-sized hole inside me with a sense of pride and self-esteem. How wrong I was. Not only had I never stopped to be grateful that I was asked to provide entertainment for the conference or to thank God for keeping me sober so I could even DJ the dance, but I had also never stopped to consider that everyone is entitled to their own opinion.

Not everybody is going to like me or like what I have to offer, even in AA. What matters is that I like myself enough to continue to take my inventory, show up for AA, work with a sponsor on trimming back my defects of character and give it all over to God and be of maximum service to my fellows.

Shortly after this awakening, I was able to shake hands with the man who made the comment about the music I played. Just days later, I sit here, thankful to God and that man for teaching me another beautiful lesson. I pray I not only strive to live the motto, "To thine own self be true," but to allow others to do the same.

Kiko M.
West Chester, Pennsylvania

What's It Worth?

April 2018

As I write in my journal, the television has to be on. I'm a "Law & Order: Criminal Intent" fanatic now that I'm not a whiskey fanatic. But mostly, I need the TV on for a little white noise in the background.

In an odd turn of events, one day I happened to find the only hour of the month that my TV show isn't on one of the 1,000 cable channels. So I scanned up and down and landed on a questionable piece of mind-candy about people who make some sort of career bidding on storage units abandoned by their owners. It failed to become my white noise: I was pulled into the drama of the junk we keep.

These men and women spent a considerable amount of currency on some assortment of broken toys and old heirlooms hidden in shadows under the dust of years of storage.

The moment of discovery is captured as the fortunate winner starts to inventory the possessions and assign them value. It's an at best arbitrary and certainly dubious mission of fact-finding.

"A box of 45 rpm records! Jackpot! $1,000 easily."

"A broken 1950s tennis racket? I can get $50 for that."

"A rusted bike wheel ... hmm ... I think it's worth $100."

At various times, I've looked at the process of my own Fourth Step inventory as being akin to emptying a clown car at the circus, a more traditional business inventory, or something in between. Now, I also see some similarities to this oddly fascinating storage unit TV show.

Each of us has an investment of emotional currency we put into all the items archived in the storage locker between the left ear and the right. Some of the merchandise we discover among our list of resentments, guilt and anger are the obvious ones. Others are long-buried pieces we discover after fearlessly and thoroughly digging into the storage. What's revealing most of all is the value we place on each item. It must have meant something or else we wouldn't still carry it around, right?

In reality, when we look at the inventory and the things we discovered, most of it falls into the category of the broken tennis racket. We hung onto it, hung onto a resentment or an idea that hanging onto it somehow made it worth something. But it wasn't worth hanging onto after all, wasting all that space and emotional currency. The guilt and long-held feuds were not the box of records of some value. We drank over life's junky, busted sports equipment and rusty bike wheels, unworthy of a penny or a minute of our time.

Scott S.
Burlington, Wisconsin

To Value You More
April 2021

In my Monday evening Women's Step Study, our small group's routine is to go around the room, giving each person the opportunity to read a paragraph or share or simply introduce herself and pass.

It happened that when it was my turn at a recent meeting, the paragraph I read was about the Fourth Step in our *Twelve Steps and Twelve Traditions* book. The paragraph is about egomania and indirectly urges us to be "a friend among friends … a worker among workers …"

In my copy of the book, that section has been underlined and highlighted in several colors of ink, revealing numerous readings over the years. I even drew stars and brackets marking specific words. Across the top of the page, at some point in the past, I scrawled the phrase: "A friend among friends … a worker among workers."

Through more than 31 years in sobriety, that paragraph has been one of the most significant anywhere in our literature for me. As I see it, those words mean that I need to humble myself, that I need to tamp down my ego. I am not the smartest kid in the room, and I need to stop acting as though I am. I need to stop judging everyone else (and finding them all lacking in some way or another). I need to be, as my sponsor used to say, just one of the many "bozos on the bus." In other words, a friend among friends, a worker among workers.

But that day, when I read that personally powerful paragraph in our meeting, the words seemed different. Suddenly the meaning of those two phrases changed for me.

To be a friend among friends and a worker among workers does not mean I value myself less than others; it means I value you more. It does not mean that my self-esteem decreases; it means that my esteem for you increases.

Another line in the same paragraph reads, "Always we tried to struggle to the top of the heap, or to hide underneath it." That made it sound like my choice was to either see myself on the top of the heap or on the bottom. But as I read those words in the meeting, I realized I was misinterpreting that too.

We are "the heap," all jumbled together, each with value, esteem and worth. In this human heap, there's no mentally healthy top or bottom for me. All this time I've been trying to figure out my "level" in the heap, when I could have been enjoying the miracle of just being in the heap at all.

As I come up on my 32nd AA birthday, people outside the Fellowship occasionally ask why I still go to "those meetings." It would be hard to explain to them, but my rereading of this single paragraph explains it in crystal clear terms to me: It's because I still have so much to learn and so much growing to look forward to.

S.J.

The Woodlands, Texas

STEP FIVE

Admitted to God, to ourselves, and to another human being
the exact nature of our wrongs.

————————◆————————

D espite a popular reputation as being loose-lipped, most alcoholics live (and sometimes die) with their secrets closely
held. Revealing them to your sponsor, a clergy person or a
loved one is a little scary but incredibly liberating, as the stories
in this chapter relate. As Snow P. writes in "The Secrets We Share,"
"... telling another alcoholic who you really are, what you have
done, what you are ashamed of, what you are proud of, what you
regret, what you need forgiveness for and what is haunting you
freed me in a way that nothing or no one else could."

Pop That Top!

May 2014

As a newcomer, I was frightened at the thought that I was going to have to spill my guts to strangers who told me I was "as sick as my secrets." I also heard that I couldn't stay sober unless I did what was called a Fifth Step—asap.

It didn't seem to register with people who had gotten through that terrible ordeal themselves that I was more than afraid to share my story. So I white-knuckled it for three whole years because I just couldn't trust people or trust the process. I don't know how I stayed sober that long. I couldn't see that people around me were getting better and I was not. After a while, it became harder and harder to go to AA meetings. I felt like a bottle of pop that had been shaken hard. My contents, already under pressure, were going to burst at the first opportunity to "blow." The people who wanted me to talk had no idea what they were asking for.

But I was scared. So at some point I decided to twist the cap of the soda bottle and see if I could release some of the gases. I sat down and actually wrote some Fourth Step memories. At first it was a disorganized mess. Yet, there was truth—a first for me. I soon began to write like a crazy person whose shirttail was on fire. Stuff came out of me that I'd thought was long ago lost forever. I kept going, thank the Higher Power!

Soon my sponsor and I made an appointment to meet. I gave her my hodgepodge of notes to look at beforehand so she could try to prepare for the mess that was sure to happen when we removed my bottled-up pop cap. To her credit, she took the crappy notes with a straight face and said she would circle things she wanted us to talk about. Her calm response was the first moment I thought there was a chance we both might live through my Fifth Step.

The day we met was sunny and springy. We sat on a park bench along the Delaware River. I wondered if I might leap into the river and drown myself if things went badly, but she assured me it was going to be AOK. We said the Serenity Prayer and she twisted my bottle cap off a bit by plunging into my notes and asking questions. The experience was intense. We could have been on a park bench on the moon for all I knew. Things spewed out unedited. And best of all, I learned that my soda bottle does have a bottom.

The other thing I learned was that I actually recognized whether I was telling the truth or fabricating some lies (which I had always been good at, since I loved a good story). My sponsor asked questions about the questionable things I said, and through that long afternoon she helped me to sort everything out. Soon I reached the bottom of my bottle.

Gratitude that my sponsor didn't quit on me in the middle of the mess I'd handed her was the only sticky residue of that afternoon on the park bench by the river. Her gift to me of her time and patience was priceless. God bless my sponsor, Nancy.

Becky G.
Greater Levittown, Pennsylvania

Sharing Everything
May 2021

I was not spiritual growing up; the concept of God was nonexistent for me. My parents grew up in very different religious traditions. They raised me in a nonreligious but spiritually open-minded way of life.

In my mind, I was certain that there was no God because when I saw people with mental and physical disabilities, I thought such conditions were too unfair for there to be a God.

When I came to AA I was offended by the spiritual aspect of the program. I just wanted to get sober! The beginning of my spirituality,

I believe, started when I heard these hard-to-believe inspirational stories from the staff of my rehab. That's when I realized I was meant to be there. But who, I wanted to know, meant for me to be there?

After moving to California to enter sober living, I quickly acquired a sponsor and started the Steps because, when sober, I discovered that I am quite good at following directions. Even so, I didn't truly believe in a Higher Power until I did my Fifth Step and shared my life story with my sponsor.

The spiritual experience I had that day is something I will never forget. By that time I had been praying for a couple of weeks, even though I was not fond of it. Then, on the morning of the day I did my Fifth Step, I got the idea of praying for my Higher Power to give me signs of his existence.

My sponsor picked me up around noon and we went to a local park where people were walking their dogs. On this beautiful day in southern California, we sat down on a sun-bleached wooden bench. Over the next few hours, I shared my fearless moral inventory with this man I didn't know all that well. I didn't then understand the nature of the Steps' promises. I was really surprised that I would feel magically relieved and forgiving afterward.

When we were done, my sponsor told me that I should go and meditate for one hour so I could reflect on the work I had done so far and to see whether there was anything more I needed to add.

After my sponsor dropped me off at home, I rode my bike back to the same park for my meditation. When I arrived, I saw another sponsor and sponsee doing Step work while sitting on the very same sun-bleached bench that my sponsor and I had sat on earlier. They must have arrived minutes after we had left.

As I meditated on the day's events, I realized that something out there heard me pray that morning. I began to feel at peace with myself and my sobriety and felt a satisfying feeling, like finishing a nice Thanksgiving dinner with family. I was now convinced my Higher Power was watching out for me. It still is to this day.

This spiritual experience taught me that I'm never alone on my path in sobriety. Spiritual change is inevitable; accepting it is the best thing I can do.

Julian S.
Huntington Beach, California

A Day at the Museum
May 2018

It was a cold and stormy morning when I awoke. Getting my kids to school as a stay-at-home sober mom was much easier now. Of course, when I was drunk, it was a nearly impossible task. And let me not forget to mention that we lived directly across the street from school!

On this particular day, I was getting to chaperone a field trip to the Art Institute of Chicago. I had been to the museum before with my kids, as my mom had a lifetime membership for our family to use. But during my drinking days, trying to get three kids, age 5 and under, to the museum with a double hangover was impossible. One time I had tried to take them, the kids had to pick me up when I fell down walking up the museum steps.

A few days before today's field trip, I had completed my Fifth Step with my sponsor. I have to say it was a spiritual experience. When my sponsor came to the house that morning to do it, all my kids just kind of disappeared and took a nap. Now that was a miracle!

When I got sober in 1993, I had no help with childcare and would take my kids to AA meetings so I could get one in every day. Those oldtimers at the New Valentine clubhouse welcomed not only me but my kids as well. We sat at a back table and they colored and I listened, Monday through Friday, 10 A.M. They bought my kids coloring books and crayons, and one member, Gene, always had some extra change and gave it to me, saying, "Stop off at the store and get the kids a treat."

After I got my two younger children to school, I met up with my older daughter's class and did service with the other parents at the school. And I thought about how, when I was drinking, I'd spent days peering out the venetian blinds of our home, watching the other parents and always feeling less than.

This day at the museum though, I had a group of five girls, all around 8 years old. My biggest challenge was not to lose any of them. We boarded the Archer Avenue bus and headed into downtown Chicago, about 20 minutes away. It was the same bus that took me to my first meeting of AA.

When we boarded the bus, I got the overwhelming feeling that I was in a safe place. It was sort of a magical moment. My Fourth Step had seemed to put me in a position of neutrality. I no longer felt the need to be at the top of the heap or to see myself as hiding underneath it.

As I looked around the bus and my eyes scanned my fellow riders, I realized we all were the same. I felt in that moment as though I had joined the human race, that I was connected with my fellow human beings in a way I hadn't been before. It was the end of isolation and the beginning of my new life. And wouldn't you know it, I even spotted another member of AA. The Fifth Step had allowed me to feel the presence of God. I always knew he was there, but I had lost him along the way.

I have to say chaperoning for my daughter's class was the start of many more similar events in my sobriety. And I'm happy to say that I did not lose any children in my group that day, nor did I fall up or down the steps of the Art Institute.

Diane D.
Chicago, Illinois

The Secrets We Share
May 2022

'I've always believed that it doesn't matter how you do the Steps, just so long as you do them. My brain damage, youth and inability to comprehend this new sober language along with my persistent disease seemed to thwart my every effort to do them. I made many fumbles, false starts, off-task attempts, and these efforts failed, but I never stopped trying to get the Steps done. With the kindness and patience of people in AA, I persevered and eventually completed the Steps over a few years.

I'm sitting in a hotel in Barcelona right now reflecting on this as I look down and see the beaded bracelet a young girl who I once sponsored made for me. The bracelet's black beads still shine and the wings and cross on it still look new.

Although I can't remember my sponsee's name right now, I remember the most important lesson I learned from her. We went through the first four Steps together. When we moved onto the Fifth Step, she said she wanted to do it with a priest or a minister. It was the first time I had heard a request like that, but I didn't think twice in helping her find someone. I took her to a female minister whom I had heard about and the appointment was made and her Fifth Step was completed. She and I worked on the rest of the Steps as best we could. It didn't take long for her to start drinking again and leave AA.

I don't know the "right" way to do the Steps. What I do know is that telling another alcoholic who you really are, what you have done, what you are ashamed of, what you are proud of, what you regret, what you need forgiveness for and what is haunting you freed me in a way that nothing or no one else could.

AA is the great equalizer. When you work the Steps in AA, you become a member of what I call a "love army," and that means you can help another alcoholic when no one else can, even someone from your "real" life who may know you well and may see you all the time. In the AA Fellowship, we can share the story of what we have done and how we did it and that's not something we will necessarily be able to share with other people in a church. That is my personal experience from working with sponsees.

One of my beautiful "pigeons," who I sponsored for years and did the Steps with, decided to tell me a secret on her deathbed. This was something she'd left out of the Fifth Step she had done with me. With the grace of God, I was able to tell her that I had done the same thing, and only my sponsor knew what I had done from my own Fifth Step. We both cried and she said she felt a peace beyond words. She died with her sobriety, her soul relieved and her blue eyes sparkling.

There is something so holy about our sharing our Fifth Steps. I still believe any way you can get started is good, but ultimately, the way members did it 80-something years ago seems to be the best way.

I get on a ship today with 70 other alcoholics in recovery to sail around the Mediterranean. For today, we have all completed our Steps in a way that allows us enough gratitude and joy to show up for our own lives and each other's and travel the world in complete freedom. How amazing is that?

Snow P.
Boca Raton, Florida

Up in Smoke
May 2013

I've never really understood the difference between regular honesty and rigorous honesty, but I'm pretty sure it has something to do with the degree of disclosure. I recently completed my Fourth and Fifth Steps with my new sponsor, a man I've come to trust enough to reveal my deepest darkest secrets to. Larry is a real "nuts and bolts" kind of AA oldtimer, who demands that his sponsees do things his way.

One of the first things he said to me was, "Pat, you've been trying to do things your way for quite a while now, and what has it gotten you? Why don't you try doing things my way just this once and see what happens?"

I couldn't argue with his reasoning at all, because I'd been in and out of AA for 40 years, and I was still trying to achieve "long-term sobriety." My main problem was that I'd never had a sponsor I trusted completely and so I'd never done a fearless and thorough Fourth and Fifth Step. The challenge of baring my soul completely to God and another human being and revealing the exact nature of my wrongs was going to take the kind of rigorous honesty that I'd never had the courage to attempt before.

I think God put Larry in my life for a reason because I knew that I could trust him and that he wouldn't be shocked or judgmental about any aspect of my past. Once I had committed myself to being rigorously honest, I was surprised at how fast and easy the work actually was. When we did my Fifth Step, I had the distinct feeling that God was right there in the room with us. I also felt a wonderful sense of love and forgiveness.

The next morning when I awoke, I felt there was something missing. It suddenly dawned on me that all the stress and anxiety and guilt I had been living with for so long was gone.

I rent a townhouse on the edge of town, and out back is a paved road about half a mile long that doesn't go anywhere. Someone had planned to develop the property a long time ago, but for some reason they never did. It's where I go to exercise and pray and listen to music with headphones. It's perfect for that because there is never any traffic or distractions—just the beautiful flora and fauna of Southern Louisiana.

The morning after my Fifth Step I gathered up the paperwork of my Fourth Step, my first ever attempt at complete and rigorous honesty. I took it out to the end of the road that leads to nowhere, crinkled it up and set it on fire. As I watched the smoke rising from the mudhole that contained the putrid essence of my past life, I felt the presence of God smiling down on me from the beautiful blue Louisiana sky. I knew without a doubt that God was filling that void inside me with love and forgiveness and the strength and desire to help others. Then I turned around and walked back down that road toward home, a new man.

Patrick K.
Baton Rouge, Louisiana

Just Listening
May 2017

I rolled out of bed onto my knees this morning. I asked the God of my understanding for his will for me. I thought about the day ahead. Tonight I would be doing something I had never done before. I would be listening to another woman's Fifth Step. This woman was someone I had never met. She was currently in an alcoholic treatment center.

I prayed for her. I asked God to fill me with his love and let me be a channel to send his love to her. I asked for her to have the courage to say what she needed to say. I prayed about the Fifth Step throughout the day. I want to be able to convey God's love. Because of what I've seen and felt, I have no doubts about his love. Even when I think I don't feel it at all, I still know it's there.

I asked God several times if I could be allowed to give her an insight into the beauty and depth of his love. I realize I don't actually know the width and depth of God's love. But I know it's great.

When I met the woman to do her Fifth Step, I liked her right away. I could see she had her brave face on. That "muscle through it" face. I saw myself in her face.

We started with prayer. I began by thanking God for loving us so much. God was most definitely present. When she got to the point in her story where her life went seriously wrong, I was thinking I could not relate. My life had not been anything like hers. I started praying to myself. I told God I couldn't relate. I didn't know what to say. I quietly asked him to please help me help her, to put the right words in my mouth, the right thoughts in my head.

What came to me immediately was ... wait ... just listen ... let her do this ... settle down ... just listen. So I did.

Soon I realized that her pain was the same as mine. Our pain had been brought about by only slightly different circumstances. Apart from details, we were the same. Betrayal, abuse, neglect, abandonment—the same. The determination, the search, the failures—the same. Anger, resentment, retaliation, confusion, mistakes, bad decisions, lost hopes, lost dreams, lost cause, trying to cope in a world gone horribly wrong—all the same. My pain was not unique.

For me, this was huge. We identified with each other. We were human. We weren't separate; we became closer. It gave me grace and forgiveness. It gave me mercy and compassion. It helped me just be me and let her be her. I could see that we were both just trying to cope the best we could.

When the woman finished her story, I talked a little bit about my life and my own experiences. She saw that we had the same stuff. I could see her relief. I could see her relax. We both knew we were not alone. If it's possible for one person to relay to another the love of God, then I was indeed allowed to do so that night. We were one alcoholic relating to another.

When I left her, I said, "It was a very good night." She turned and looked at me and smiled and said, "Yes, it was."

I don't know if she'll be able to maintain sobriety. That's not up to me. But I do know she saw a glimpse into a different life tonight and that everything happened exactly the way it was supposed to. For her and for me.

Kathryn W.
Chancellor, Alabama

STEP SIX

Were entirely ready to have God remove all these
defects of character.

———————◆———————

Asking a Higher Power to remove our "defects" (think exces-
sive fear, anger, pride, judgement, or overindulgence in
areas other than alcohol) that we uncovered in Step Four
is an important Step and, as Nicholas L. writes in his story
"PRO.CRAS.TIN.A.TION," needs to be preceded by being "entirely
willing to change and grow." As the authors found in this chapter
can attest, Step Six is the beginning of letting go of behaviors we
once considered necessary for protection and even survival—but
in fact inhibit our happiness as we move deeper into sobriety.

Letting Go
June 2017

For a long time I thought Step Six meant doing nothing, just waiting around and being ready. I wondered why it had to be a separate Step. Why not just go ahead to Step Seven and ask?

But one day, during my morning meditation, I was plagued by one of my defects and realized there is an action to take in Step Six. Being entirely ready means letting go. That's my part. Right in the middle of a bad thought or attitude or action—if I recognize it—I can stop it right then, without completing it, without giving myself that satisfaction. And I might have to do this over and over. I might have to because certain defects are, in some strange way, comfortable, familiar, even pleasurable.

Maybe I'm the only one who nurses some of my defects—but I don't think so, from what I've heard at my AA meetings. It seems like we all do it. Isn't there a song with the lyric, "Hurts so good"? That's what I'm talking about.

Somehow when it comes to me, though, my defect always seems so understandable, absolutely justified: No one cares about me. My feelings are hurt. Poor me. Why does this always happen to me? Why does everyone do this to me?

As I once heard at a recovery retreat, the way to deal with a defect is to break in and say "Stop it!" when I am obsessing on it. Just stop—and let it go. Easier said than done, of course.

I sometimes think of letting go as releasing a colorful balloon into the sky. Like a child, I don't want to lose it; I have the string tied tightly around my finger. But if I want to be free, I have to let that cherished thing float up to the sky. It looks so light as it floats up, but it's really a heavy harness on my neck, keeping me tethered to old ways that don't work anymore. It actually feels so much better when it's gone.

So here's where I try to do my part. I say to myself, "Stop it. Let it go," right in the middle of doing it if I can. Stop thinking that thought or talking about that person for the millionth time. Stop dragging myself down. Then I ask my Higher Power to help me.

I can't say that I ever do this perfectly. But like the rest of us, I keep trying.

Lynne D.
Carbondale, Illinois

Deadly Sins
June 2022

The Seven Deadly Sins of pride, greed, lust, anger, gluttony, envy and sloth are mentioned in our literature. This list has been very helpful to me as I have repeatedly trudged through my past while working my Steps. Each sin has served as a convenient guide during my search of past activities dating back into my high school years. Looking back, I see that I was a pretty normal kid—until I started drinking alcohol.

My first drink was just a sip from a can of beer offered by an older person in my family as we were parked in front of a store that sold television sets. We were poor and hadn't purchased a TV yet. Yes, that was quite a few years ago. That small amount of alcohol made me feel excited and my nose started itching. I remember when we got home, I grabbed a mirror to look at my nose. I dropped the mirror and broke it. Maybe that was a bad omen of my future drinking.

Taking pride in my ability to mooch a drink from other students soon led to greed for more than my share. Occasionally we gave a few bucks to someone at the local pool hall so they would buy us some booze. I had a part-time job fueling cars and this job gave me the opportunity to drain gasoline from the hoses between customers. We used that gas to drive around. And while we were driving around on country dirt roads, we would siphon gas from tractors parked out in the fields. Occasionally, an angry bull would add to our adventure.

There was one episode back in those days that scares me every time I remember it. My "drinking-thinking" had led me into justifying theft if the object of the theft was something the owner, in my opinion, had plenty of or didn't need or wasn't using. My car was in the shop one night, so four friends and I drove a loaner car down a busy highway going 80 mph. We were all drinking. My friends were taking turns pointing an old 16-gauge shotgun out the window toward other cars and pulling the trigger.

We had found the shotgun earlier in an old, abandoned farmhouse. It had a corroded shotgun shell in it and the shell appeared to have already been used, but we couldn't remove it from the barrel. We had pulled the trigger a dozen times to make sure it had already been discharged. As we drove around drinking more, someone pointed the end of the barrel at the floor under my seat. That was when the gun fired. The loud noise was terrifying! And the realization of what we could have done was terrifying. The car was new with plush carpeting on the floor, and now the carpeting had a big hole in it. We used our pocket combs to hide the hole before returning the car to the dealer.

I'm not proud of the events in those early days of my alcoholic drinking. Neither am I proud of the other "deadly sins" I was involved with during more than 30 years of active alcoholism. I am, however, extremely proud of my 28 years as an AA member and of my past involvement in AA service.

My indulgence in greed still drives me at times. Sometimes I find myself arriving to meetings early, before the donuts from the previous meeting are all eaten. And I can get a bit angry when my gluttony for AA coffee cannot be fulfilled. Envy was one of my reasons for heavy drinking in the past and it has, over time, been replaced by a sense of gratitude for the peace of mind I now have.

And sloth? I'll consider that one after my sobriety nap.

Glenn P.
Florissant, Missouri

Defects, What Defects?

June 2016

I remember walking into an AA meeting at the Tri-County Center almost two years ago. I told myself, I'm not like these people. I don't have a problem. I was scared and mentally and physically drained after having just been released from a detox. I quietly made my way into the meeting room.

What I now know to be the Twelve Steps were hanging near the chair where I sat. I read them and thought to myself that I had worked at least eight of the Steps already. I assumed that the others would not be that hard. I knew I could easily knock them out in a few days, if I tried hard. I thought there would be a few Steps I could avoid or disregard. I read Step Six: "Were entirely ready to have God remove all these defects of character."

What defects? I thought. I am perfect and could not possibly have any defects. Even if I did have flaws, to remove them all would make me boring and no fun to be around. I didn't realize that no one wanted to be around me anyway because my drinking had caused so much pain for others. My behavior caused my phone calls to go unanswered. Doors were never opened when I knocked. Life had become unbearable, not just for me, but for those I considered my friends. My defects had become my assets. Manipulation, lying and deception were just the top three picks on my long list of defects.

After completing my Fifth Step with my sponsor, I was instructed to make a list of my defects. I was told to arrange them in order from most used to those less frequently used. Until then, I hadn't realized that I had been using these defects against myself as well. I manipulated my thoughts to fit any circumstance in order to deceive my own brain. I lied to myself about what I thought was right.

I came to many realizations through working the Steps. For example,

Step Six is not about making me into a robot. I don't have to do everything right. I just have to change my thinking and allow myself to ask my Higher Power to guide me through the day. I want this Higher Power to allow me to make the right decisions.

The smallest of tasks, I now found, those which used to puzzle me, could be done with ease if I just asked. Step Six is not about making a blood sacrifice or announcing my defects over the mall intercom, but quietly and in a most sincere way, asking for help. I must be submissive in asking for change, rather than being a dominant, overbearing narcissist trying to control every thought and action.

When faced with obstacles that seem to baffle me, I ask for help, and those defects of character will soon be diminished—if I'm willing. Here's a prayer that helps me: "God, thank you for removing my fear and for showing me the truth about myself. I need your help to become willing to let go of the things in me which continue to block me off from you. Please grant me your grace, and make me willing to have these objectionable characteristics, defects and shortcomings removed."

Anonymous

PRO.CRAS.TIN.A.TION
June 2021

This morning I sat down at my desk, which is inundated with papers that have been building into heaps over the two years since my ex-wife ceased doing my paperwork. Looking at the pile, I thought about one of my pronounced defects of character—procrastination. Some people call that a five-syllable word for sloth.

Procrastination keeps me from cleaning up my desk and keeps me from doing everything I need to do to improve my little business's profitability and restore my diminished finances. Thanks to AA, this kind of thinking squirreled through my brain for only about 15 seconds. I was then reminded that in the four years and four months I've been in the program, I've successfully used the Steps and followed the advice given in our Big Book.

Each of the four times I've worked the Steps, I have received the gift of having one of my most severe defects of character removed, notably one that hurts me, such as fear. Some of these were long-standing defects that for most of my life I had been unable to control. Each of these defects were addressed in the order that my mental and physical health—not my finances—required at the time. My addiction to alcohol and other drugs was lifted; my reliance on others to validate my sense of self-worth was lifted; problems I've had with many of my relationships were lifted; and problems related to food are in the process of being lifted.

One by one, the behaviors that hurt me most have been lifted. And each time I did the Steps, I made myself entirely willing to change and grow. And each time I received a helping hand from the loving Higher Power I've met through AA.

I remember when I received my one-month chip, I said, "I feel like this is the first time I've ever really earned something." So many things—material and genetic—were gifted to me by my parents, but this relief from character defects was all due to my own hard work on the Steps.

When I thought this morning about why my defect of sloth had not yet been lifted, I realized it's still with me because I'm able to function despite it. My business still plugs along; I have four or five happy employees who enjoy coming to work, who can provide for their families; I have enough to eat and a place to sleep; and I have friends.

Since I had not yet started my latest round of working the Steps to address my powerlessness over this sloth, I have faith that when I do, I'll have a very good chance of being relieved of it. I know that because the Steps have always worked for me.

I've yet to hear someone in the thousands of AA meetings I've attended complain that they tried working the program fearlessly and thoroughly only to find it didn't work.

As I said my prayers and meditated this morning, I thanked God for the defects from which I have already been released. I thanked God for not waving a magic wand and making it all clear up at once, but allowing me to feel that I'm actually working to help effect positive change in my life through spiritual development.

My Higher Power has granted me the patience to savor each gift I've already obtained. I also have the serenity to hope that the rest of the Promises will materialize—sometimes quickly, sometimes slowly—if I work for them. I am incredibly lucky.

Nicholas L.
Paris

Restraint of Face
June 2020

The first time I read the Big Book, all I got out of it was that I needed to get "stuff" out of my head by writing it down. Get it "down on paper," Bill wrote. So I started writing. I should have asked for help. I would not recommend the way I went about it.

I wrote letters to everyone in my family about my alcoholism. I also mentioned that I was dating a recovering drug addict. This was in the years before email and texting. I made copies of this several-pages-long letter and mailed it out. It was supposed to be my amends letter—supposed to be. Like I said, I should have asked for help.

What happened was that the letter just did more damage to my loved ones. If I could have hit the "this message will self-destruct" button before they read it, I would have. As soon as I put them in the mail box, I knew that I shouldn't have sent them.

Over time, I have learned to ask for help, go over ideas with my sponsor about making amends and communicate with others before I act. Before AA, I had a long history of sending horribly destructive letters. Once, I even sent all the women in my family copies of the same letter telling them that they were selfish, self-serving and arrogant.

Funny, that's exactly who I was, not them. I didn't know until I did my Step work that I was projecting all the sick stuff inside me onto all the women in my life.

I was the same way with my tongue. Before AA and for the first several years in recovery, I would cut people down verbally. I always had to have the last word and I didn't stop harping on a topic until you understood (in other words ... got my way).

In my 18th year of sobriety, a woman in my home group told me to "leave them alone until you can leave them alone." What did that mean? It took me almost two decades of recovery to learn to keep my mouth shut.

I am so grateful that I learned discernment when it comes to my writing and my speaking. No one needs to read or hear the thoughts rattling around in my brain except God and a trusted sponsor. Only then, after receiving coaching and guidance from trusted advisors, can I share what I am thinking or make amends without hurting anyone.

In the past 10 years, I learned that I also must restrain my face. I learned that my facial expressions are hurtful. I finally learned, way past my teenage years, that eye-rolling, sighing, sideways glances, head tilting and harrumphing can hurt people.

When talking to my daughter about this newfound awareness, she questioned me. "Are you supposed to cover up or lie about your feelings and not express them?"

"No," I replied. "It's not about lying, not expressing or covering up. It's about having discernment, paying attention to my face."

Not everyone in an AA meeting or out in public needs to know that I'm bored, dissatisfied, exhausted, mad, frustrated, disgruntled or late. My face, without me consciously knowing it, once told a newcomer that I was bored with what she was saying. It was true. I was bored and the newcomer questioned me about it. Had she not confronted me, I would have never known that she noticed.

This confrontation sparked a quest for me to understand my face. When I talked with trusted AA friends about this topic, they agreed with the newcomer. They said I scared people at times. Wow. I was shocked. Talk about peeling back an onion layer.

I thank God that I now have the experience, strength and hope to address my facial-restraint issues. When I have sponsees who do what I used to do, I talk to them about it. Many times they're just as shocked as I was.

One sponsee stated, "I have a 'resting b— face.' That's my face. I am OK with that." I wasn't sure how to respond to that and said, "From me to you, I learned from trusted friends in the program that newcomers would not approach me because they feared me. That means my face didn't allow me to do Twelfth Step work. If we do not do Twelfth Step work, we die because faith without works is dead."

She looked at me and said, "It's how I keep people away from me." That was something I could understand, and we both agreed we had Step work to do on this topic.

Thank God for these Steps. This sponsee no longer has a "resting b— face." We must work these Steps in all our affairs, including what we do with our faces, whether we know we are doing it or not.

Anonymous
Milledgeville, Georgia

High and Dry
June 2019

I have spent most of my life on or around the water, where I often see those small aluminum boats. I picture one with a hundred little pinholes in its hull. A guy is fishing, and every so often, he stops to bail water out of the bilge. As new holes appear, he spends more time bailing and less time fishing. To me, these holes are like my defects of character and the water in the bilge, my shortcomings.

My vigilance today is focused on the day-to-day issues of my life and my motives for how I handle those issues. Either I can become willing to patch those little holes, one at a time, as I become aware of them, or I can spend the rest of my life bailing water and risk sinking altogether.

Today, thanks to AA, my boat is high and dry, the fishing is great, and so is life.

Rick R.
Poway, California

STEP SEVEN

Humbly asked Him to remove our shortcomings.

———— ♦ ————

Sometimes anger flares up in a traffic jam or fear and resentment arise at work because of a casual comment from your boss. Acknowledging your own part in any situation—as April P. does in "The Ex-Mother-In-Law"—allows you to understand that others are "as human as I am." What a relief that is, since anger and fear are heavy burdens to carry! As Dana F. puts it in "One Night on a Church Playground," "I have done the Seventh Step more than once, and each time I do ... I find new, sober, and estimable ways to behave that allow me to move gently through each day." John P. in "Speaking of Humility" recalls how an event at a meeting opened his eyes. "I could explain humility, but I was not actually living it," he writes, adding that the meeting "pushed me to work on my spiritual fitness, improve how I monitor my shortcomings, and remember to ask for God's help in removing them."

One Night on a Church Playground
July 2014

had no idea that on January 21, 1999 my life was going to change forever. I was barely 15 years old and terrified I was going to die a horrific alcoholic death. I had been coming to AA and taking the suggestions, but my desire to drink overpowered the one to stay sober. So many nights I had promised my parents I would stay dry, but I got drunk despite my best intentions.

But on January 20, I got drunk for what I pray was the last time. I cried as I confessed my slip to my family and peers at my therapy group. I then rushed to an AA meeting, and while sitting there that day, I felt the grace of a Higher Power enter my spirit. I chose to believe because I wanted to have faith that this solution could work for me.

So why did I keep getting drunk if I was going to meetings, praying and calling other women in the program? Why did I have no defense after months of AA? Members of my home group had warned me about "people, places and things," but they didn't know what it was like to try to change all your friends as a high school freshman. But I finally realized they were right and began to listen.

I started going to 90 meetings in 90 days and drove with my home group all over New York to outgoing commitments. And I started doing the Steps right out of the Big Book. My sponsor Amy was the same age as my mother, but I respected her program. At young people's meetings, it was easier to focus on boys, chain smoking (since we were still able to smoke in meetings), or the next party—so I needed the stability of oldtimers in my life. Slowly, things started to improve. But it was when I got to Step Seven that I began to really see and feel a change. I still consider Step Seven my favorite Step.

When I did Step Five with Amy, we were able to identify my patterns and behaviors. We made a list of my defects, and I went home and sat quietly for an hour making sure I was ready to move on. She felt I was holding on to some old behaviors and made me sit with Six and Seven for a period. Finally the pain of becoming "entirely ready" became unbearable. She was right. I didn't exactly want to stop stealing; I didn't want to stop sleeping around; I didn't want to start going to all my classes. Frankly, some of my defects still felt good. I certainly didn't want to have to start paying for things! Making changes was scary and hard. I was reluctant to try to start living a different way. I had no idea how or where to begin.

For the next few weeks, I acted out with my character defects. And I was painfully aware of exactly what I was doing as I was doing it. When I stole something, I knew it was wrong and I felt guilty. I felt regret after casual encounters with boys, and I began to recognize when they treated me poorly. When I had a fight and cursed at my parents, I felt remorse and saw how my actions hurt those around me. While sitting in Step Six, I came again to a jumping off point, but this time it was in sobriety. I felt if I didn't do exactly as my sponsor asked me, I would surely drink again.

One Wednesday night at the Leonard Park Group, I sat outside on the church's playground and cried and cried. I began to pray. I got up and called my sponsor and told her I was ready to have a Higher Power remove all these defects of character. As with Step One, my surrender had to be complete if I expected to continue in AA. Again, I made the choice to believe that the people in the rooms had a solution that could work for me. My sponsor and I came up with a list of substitute behaviors and traits that I could employ rather than defaulting to my self-destructive ones.

The effects I felt were immediate, and this is what I love about Step Seven. I could actually see what was changing in me. For months people in AA were telling me I looked and sounded better, but I didn't really feel any better. Once I started changing the way I behaved, my growth became visible. I felt different. I felt sober.

I want to be clear: I did not take the Seventh Step and miraculously become a better person. I have battled with different incarnations of the same character defects throughout my entire sobriety. However, since that Wednesday night long ago, I think I have taken every single suggestion a sponsor has given me. Sometimes I kick and scream, but I do as I'm asked because I know that these women have my best interests at heart. I have done the Seventh Step more than once, and each time I do, I feel the freedom of surrendering these defects. I find new, sober and estimable ways to behave that allow me to move gently through each day.

Today is my anniversary, and it is a relief to reflect on these last 15 years and celebrate all the changes. I am not the girl who came in here. I am a young woman who is filled with hope and does her best to carry that light into the world around me.

Dana F.
Warren, Rhode Island

An Unfamiliar Inner Peace
July 2022

When I sobered up this last time, my original sponsor coached me on the Seventh Step. He and other members of my home group talked about doing favors, helping others and not getting caught. We were told that doing the right thing and not taking or getting credit for it was good practice toward humility, a key feature of the Step.

Though not stated this way in the Big Book, we talked about character defects being about those things we do that we shouldn't do. And Step Seven is about doing those things we should be doing but are not. For me, cheating, stealing and lying are behaviors I need to give up. Arriving at work on time, giving my employer a day's work for a day's pay, coming home for dinner instead of going to the bar, providing love and comfort to my family—all these and others are the actions I truly need to attend to. My more religious friends might call these things sins of commission or sins of omission. Either way, it became clear to me that I needed to focus on these markers of my character.

My great-grandsponsor told us that AA is a way of life in which drinking alcohol is no longer necessary. If I embrace this way of life and do the work, the alcohol problem will simply be lifted, as is promised in the Tenth Step.

Early in sobriety, I decided to go back to school. The classes I took were held at night, starting at about 5:30 P.M. This meant that I had to park near the campus by 5:15 or so to get to class on time. One day, I parked in a metered spot. The meter's sign said it needed to be fed until 6:00 P.M; after that time, the spot was free. My glove box contained ignored parking tickets and other traffic summonses. I figured, What does one more mean, one way or the other? and started off down the sidewalk to class. After taking several steps, I stopped. I thought about what my sponsor had been trying to teach me about the Seventh Step. I don't know what got into me, but I went back and put enough money in the meter to get me through to 6:00 P.M.

As I walked away, an odd new sensation went through me. I felt strangely empowered, with an unfamiliar inner peace. My new sense of myself was that I could be someone who does his duty, one who is a contributing member of society. I stood there and chuckled to myself. For a few cents I got to feel this good? What a deal.

That was a beginning for me in using Step Seven to improve my life. Over the years, I have added lots of little actions that no one would notice, actions I don't get credit for. I look for opportunities to simply make the world slightly better—picking up after myself, letting people pull in to the traffic lane. These seemingly trivial acts calm me, give me the feeling that I'm adding back rather than selfishly taking, as I did during my drinking years. It's a good feeling, one that adds little sparks of joy to my day.

This Seventh Step work brought me to a dramatic turning point in my attitude. A friend and I were having lunch at a cafe with outdoor seating. Our table adjoined a busy street that was under construction. There were four lanes, two going in each direction, with concrete barriers separating the opposing lanes. An elderly lady driver turned the wrong way into two lanes where heavy city traffic was coming at her head-on. There was much honking and blinking of headlights from the oncoming cars. She was petrified and froze, her hands gripping the wheel. She stopped her car, blocking both lanes.

My friend and I looked up from our lunches, slightly amused by the spectacle. Suddenly from an adjoining table, a beautiful young woman, dressed fashionably in a business suit, stood, kicked off her high heels and vaulted over the curbside barrier. She held out both hands to halt the traffic. She turned to the paralyzed lady and helped her perform a series of turns that got her headed out of trouble. With the lady on her way, the woman turned, waved the traffic on, vaulted back over the barrier and resumed eating her salad.

To this day, I envy that young woman. I want what she has. I want that instinct to stand up and help. I want that "inspiration, an intuitive thought or a decision" that's promised in our Big Book. I want my service to others to be so instinctive that I can respond like that woman did when the opportunity comes.

The Big Book says that our purpose in doing this work is to "fit ourselves to be of maximum service to God and the people about us." Practicing the Seventh Step the way I was taught may someday bring me to her admirable level.

T.T.

Albuquerque, New Mexico

Drama Queen

July 2016

When I got to AA, I thought if I could just stop drinking it would solve all my problems. Drinking alcoholically certainly was my most glaring defect; but over time, others rose to the surface. It has taken time for me to see how my character defects and shortcomings negatively affected my sobriety. However, now I've discovered that with alcohol removed, anger leads the parade.

Today, I've been sober almost half my life, and I'm grateful for the progress and growth I have experienced in Alcoholics Anonymous. But growth has been slow in many areas. I have learned my "old ideas" are the place where my defects of character reside. For them to be removed, I must humbly seek and act on our spiritual solution.

Only a few years ago, I was able to begin making headway with anger. Certainly I wanted my anger and the consequences of anger to be gone, but I kept exerting my willpower rather than relying on our Steps. Humiliation brought me to the threshold of Steps Six and Seven, and humility allowed me to cross over. Powerlessness forced my surrender.

An argument with my daughter was the catalyst that awoke me to a spiritual experience. Having the right motives paired with bad behavior just does not work. The damage spread as phone calls and voice messages were left for other family members. Finally, I paused and went for a walk, shaking with anger. It took a long time to calm down enough so I could begin to see my mistakes.

First I prayed, and then I called my sponsor. Whenever I talked to him about a problem his first question was always, "Did you pray about this?" Filled with humiliation, I made more phone calls, attempting to make amends.

Several hours later my wife called from work, exhausted from all the phone calls left by our daughters and me. Words of wisdom came from this wonderful and patient woman who had become an innocent victim of her husband's anger.

Calmly and dejectedly, she told me how this had disrupted her day, and then she told me something that hit me between the eyes, a truth that I had not seen about myself. She said I complained about others being "drama queens," but that I was the drama queen. Quietly, I agreed.

After the phone call, I got on my knees and truly took Steps Six and Seven concerning anger. Steps Six and Seven were not about me acting out or working on eliminating these defects, which I had tried over and over. It became necessary for me to realize my powerlessness and the unmanageability surrounding all my defects of character, and then to seek God's help in removing these defects. Humility was required as I asked him to remove my anger. My sponsor has told me many times that humility is the heart of AA. On that day, I began to not only experience it, but to develop a better understanding of what it means to turn my difficulties over to God.

How I wish that my anger was completely gone. A vast improvement has been made, though. When I remember to pause, and pray to have anger removed, I seem to do OK. Doing the right thing keeps me out of self-imposed dilemmas.

S.

Rio Rancho, New Mexico

The Ex-Mother-In-Law
July 2015

At two years sober, I wrote down my Step Seven. I prayed with my pastor and my sponsor that my shortcomings be removed. I felt as if a burden were lifted after we prayed, as if I were on that "pink cloud" all over again. I tried to convince myself that I would no longer be selfish, judgmental and impatient, that I would be able to let all my resentments float away.

A year later I still resented the same people. My biggest resentment was for my former mother-in-law. She had taken care of my kids for 10 years while I was busy getting drunk. I hated her for everything she did right, and for everything she did wrong.

My kids had ended up with her when I went to jail and their father went to rehab. My phone calls from jail went unanswered. When I got out, I didn't call very often, because I knew she wouldn't answer. I got on with my life, which entailed two more rehabs, another visit to jail and a stay in a homeless shelter. In my mind, life was an uphill battle that I just could not win.

But I wanted my kids back. I knew I would have to get sober and stay sober. Instead, I drank to forget, and the resentment got bigger and bigger.

When I got into AA, it was tough just to get myself to meetings and hold down a job. I remember sitting in meetings crying, telling everyone I just wanted to be a mother. During those first years of sobriety, I prayed for my kids. Some nights I'd be jarred out of a deep sleep by nightmares. I dreamed my kids were drowning or lost or hurt.

I didn't get to hear their voices until I had 18 months sober. That was a long 18 months. But I put myself in the center of AA. I did service work. I made coffee for my home group. I worked the Steps. I talked to other alcoholics who had been through what I was going through, and that made the pain bearable.

Recovery brings massive rewards. At three years of sobriety, a judge awarded custody of my kids back to me. My joy was quickly overshadowed by hate and thoughts of revenge. I was going to punish this woman who kept my kids away from me. I would keep her from seeing them, just like she had kept them from me.

My resentment for this woman started as a snowball and became an avalanche. I hired a lawyer to keep her away. I complained to my sponsor about her on a daily basis. I reveled in the idea that she would be alone now, never to see the kids again.

Then a judge gave her visitation rights. I bristled with anger! I stood on the porch one day talking to my sponsor on the phone about it. Finally, she told me she was done listening to it. With no one to talk to, I just paced on the porch.

Suddenly, a feeling of remorse came over me. For some reason my mind replayed the things I had done and not done during all those years she was caring for my kids. I felt grateful that she had kept them all together and not let them become wards of the state. Having seen the situations of other alcoholic parents, I knew that my kids could have had it a lot worse.

As I paced the porch that day, I remembered the words of Step Seven: "Humbly asked Him to remove our shortcomings." I remembered my prayer. A tear formed in my eye as I realized God was answering it.

I played a part in this hate. If I didn't change, nothing would change. Hatred was consuming me, stealing my serenity. I decided that I did not want to feel this way anymore. I called her and said that the judge was right, that she should see the kids. I apologized for everything I had done to her. She accepted my apology.

Today we have a good working relationship. Sometimes resentment creeps back up on me. These are the days I call her and we talk. I see she is as human as I am. Knowing now how tough motherhood is on a daily basis makes me grateful that she stepped up and did my job for 10 years. If she needs something, I am there. If her car breaks down, I offer mine. When she calls, I answer the phone. Now she gets to be the grandmother she always wanted to be, and I am OK with it, thanks to God and Step Seven.

April P.
Monongahela, Pennsylvania

Running Away
July 2016

When I was five years sober, I was walking along a road in Great Neck, Long Island, when I saw a guy coming directly toward me. This guy had once cheated me out of several thousand dollars by cashing an insurance check of mine that he had mistakenly received. And there was no reason for him not to have paid me back. Instead of confronting him, though, I chose to cross the street.

That was an AA awakening. I vowed never to do that again. Running away was not going to be an option anymore. Neither was ignoring situations or excusing other people's bad behavior, such as telling myself he needed the money more than I did.

I had always done almost anything to avoid confrontation. After all, "they" might not like me. "They" were so much more important than I was. But that day, I asked God to give me the courage not only to understand my behavior, but to overcome this character defect of mine.

An amazing part of my AA journey is discovering that when I directly handle life's problems head-on, most of them resolve quite easily. For me, courage is not only doing "the next right thing," but to begin to act appropriately. The Steps have helped me to "say what I mean, but never say it mean." Action. Step Seven. That's the key for me. No more running away.

Steve M.
Brentwood, Tennessee

Speaking of Humility
July 2018

L ast November, I volunteered to speak at a topic meeting. This would be my first speaker meeting at this group, and it would be on the Friday after Thanksgiving. I decided to speak on the topic of humility since the words "humble" and "humility" show up so often in the Big Book.

I devoted weeks to research and I learned some interesting things. The word "humility" comes from Latin, meaning "of the earth, not the heavens." Additionally, it has been argued that the Twelve Steps have their basis in humility. Further, many religions hold that humility is essential for beginning a spiritual path. Some sources even argue that humility is the one condition to receiving divine grace.

I rehearsed and reedited my lines. They were poetic, powerful even. This presentation would be seen as one of the best of the year, I thought. It might even be good enough for a regional roundup.

So on Black Friday, I went to the meeting early to check in with the group leader. However, I discovered that he was out of town. Before I could find the substitute group leader, the meeting was called to order. The meeting advanced through the usual agenda. I was feeling a little nervous, but I focused on rehearsing the lines in my head.

Finally, we were ready to get to the topic. I was coiled to spring into action as soon as my name was called. But to my shock, the substitute group leader introduced a different member, a guy named Bobby, to do the topic presentation. I was not sure whether to interrupt the meeting or let it proceed. I chose to remain silent and just grit my teeth through the meeting. The presentation by Bobby was on gratitude, since it was the Thanksgiving holiday weekend. It was excellent, but I only heard parts of it.

As I sat there, I began to realize what had happened. In the hand-off to the substitute group leader, no one had given him the list of scheduled speakers. Consequently, he called someone else to present. This was an honest mistake of little consequence. Nonetheless, I was so overcome with anger and self-pity that I hurried out after the meeting in stony silence and vowed never to return.

The next day, I was called out of town for a week. This gave me time to reflect on my resentment. The conclusion: my ego had taken over. I had turned what was supposed to be an act of service into an act of self-promotion. I had created a fantasy with grandiose outcomes. I was more interested in making an impression than making a connection with the group.

On that Black Friday, I could explain humility, but I was not actually living it. I was putting my personality over spiritual principles. This realization was, dare I say it, humbling.

It's ironic that I learned more about humility from this scheduling error than the group would have received from my presentation. I'm actually grateful this scheduling error happened. It uncovered several of my character shortcomings. It pushed me to work on my spiritual fitness, improve how I monitor my shortcomings and remember to ask for God's help in removing them.

Another thing I learned? I promise not to do a speaker meeting on this topic again until I am sure about my motivation.

John P.
Minneapolis, Minnesota

STEP EIGHT

Made a list of all persons we had harmed, and became willing to make amends to them all.

———————— ♦ ————————

Here's another Step that focuses on becoming willing, in this case by making a list of people we have hurt, especially during our drinking careers. Because we are potentially impacting other people's lives, it's important to consider our list carefully and share it with our sponsor or another trusted AA. "Recognizing that I had done harm was an important internal shift for me," writes Gail V. in "Torn Apart." "Before I was only concerned about what others had done to me." Our Eighth Step list guides us to make our amends when ready and can help us to forgive. Forgiveness, as Valerie T. says in "The Medicine My Heart Needed," helps her move toward "health, happiness and love."

Torn Apart
August 2021

Recently I was reading a story in the Steps section of Grapevine and I remembered how, in early sobriety, I learned the true meaning of the Eighth Step. What I found interesting about gaining understanding about this Step is that the lesson didn't come from a fellow member of AA. It came from my sister.

When I first heard about the Eighth Step, I understood it to mean that I would need to go around saying sorry to everyone for all the harm that I'd caused. And because I still had a lot of guilt and shame about the things I had done in my past, I almost felt like I needed to go around introducing myself, saying, "Hi, I'm sorry and I'm Gail."

The relationship I had with my sister, who's six years younger than me, had been very unhealthy. I got sober when I was 18. She was just a kid then and I had been an abusive tornado in her life.

I was about two years sober when one evening, she and I got into a verbal fight. Today I can't recall what the fight was about, and neither can she. At the time though, it was important to us. During the fight, she ran upstairs to her room and slammed the door. I instantly felt bad about my behavior toward her and how I had reacted. I didn't want to be that person anymore and I was disappointed in myself. I wanted to go up to her room and tell her that I was sorry for yelling and fighting with her, but I knew she wasn't going to listen to me.

Instead, I wrote her a letter. It was a letter of amends. In it, I did something I had never done before. I listed out a plan of action describing how I was going to change the way I behaved and the different types of tools I was going to use to implement that change.

I slid the letter under her door and went to my AA meeting. When I returned from the meeting, I found at my bedroom door my letter ripped up, with a sign saying, "I don't think so, not this time," followed by some more colorful language. My immediate impulse was to run upstairs to her room, grab her and shake her and yell, "Didn't you read the letter? I said I was sorry and that I love you!"

I didn't do that, thank God. Instead I realized it didn't matter that she didn't believe me because I didn't want to be that type of sister anymore. I decided to follow through with the plan of action that I had outlined in the letter.

I once heard someone share at a meeting that the word "amend" does not mean "to say sorry" as much as it means "to change." If I say I'm going to amend a document that means I am going to change something in it. That was the lesson I learned that day with my sister. Instead of just saying that I was sorry, I had written out for her—but mostly for me—a plan of action to change.

This realization has had a big impact on the way I now approach the Eighth Step. Not only do I look at what I've done to harm others, but I think about what I'll be doing now to change and not be that person again. Then I have to ask myself whether I'm truly ready to follow through on that plan, because nothing sucks more than having to go back and make an amend on an amend that I already made!

Please don't get me wrong. It is important to feel remorse and to apologize for harm done to others. In fact, recognizing that I had done harm was an important internal shift for me. Before I was only concerned about what others had done to me. AA, however, is a program of action and I have learned that it's action where I've found my recovery. That's where the big changes happen for me.

So now before I move on to the Ninth Step, I make sure that the plan of action that I listed in my Eighth Step is solid and realistic. I go over it with my sponsor and other close AA friends and I pray about it.

I will always be grateful for that lesson from my sister, as I feel it has improved my recovery. Sometimes we can learn valuable AA lessons from people outside of our meetings.

Gail V.
Burlington, Ontario

Ready to Sweep
August 2015

When I was an active alcoholic, I caused physical, mental and spiritual damage to people. And as my drinking became more destructive, I isolated and alienated myself from others even more than usual, in an attempt to drink and drug without interruption or negative criticism. I'd then be overwhelmed with fear, shame, guilt and remorse. My self-loathing would spill over into all my relationships—the few that still remained, that is.

The Eighth Step gave me the toolbox I needed to explore these relationships more deeply. It enabled me to pinpoint those individuals whom I had harmed. And even if I was not actually ready to make direct amends to certain people, I was able to begin by writing out an amends list and praying for the willingness.

As I worked through my list, the essential question for me, as it says in the "Twelve and Twelve," was: "Whom have I harmed?" and in what ways. I was tempted to recall and list the ways these people had hurt me. In all honesty, there was perhaps harm on both sides. But I needed to focus on the harm I had produced. The Eighth Step does not depend on the character defects and shortcomings of others. I had to admit and acknowledge my own character defects and shortcomings. I needed to focus on "sweeping my side of the street."

When feelings of defensiveness began to emerge, I remembered that these individuals needed my forgiveness just as much as I needed theirs. But whether they recognized that need was not the issue. If I were to be serious about mending broken relationships, and I certainly was, I needed to let go of my resentments and, simultaneously, to forgive others.

The following questions were helpful to me as I worked on my Eighth Step:

1) How was I bad-tempered because of my drinking?

2) Did I avoid friends and family as a result of my obsession?

3) What damage did I produce by letting my self-will run riot?

These helped me gain valuable insights and discover other people to add to my list.

As I continued on my Eighth Step journey, it became apparent that I did much damage to myself as well. And it dawned on me that the most effective amends that I could make to myself was to stay sober and practice the Steps to the best of my ability. And if I keep not drinking just for today, I won't drink for the rest of my life.

In early sobriety, I would never have contemplated making the first move toward making an amend. But now I'm attempting to discern and apply the will of God in my life. I now take responsibility for my sobriety and for my relationships. Taking such a risk has become a possibility thanks to the Steps and my support network in the rooms of AA. The Eighth Step has given me the ability to maintain and develop a deep intimacy and involvement with significant others in my life. It also gives me emotional and spiritual balance.

Gary T.
Poughkeepsie, New York

Enraged
August 2018

I had been around AA for about three years and I'd done a few inventories. I knocked some names off my amends list, but I still wasn't free. There was this one resentment that I wasn't yet willing to let go of, and I knew without a doubt that I didn't owe this guy an amends.

During my active alcoholism, I had not been the best boyfriend to the woman who's now my wife. When we were together, she had made an emotional connection with a man she worked with. When I found out about the two of them, I fully intended to go to his place of work and kill him. Luckily, that didn't happen.

This man made it onto each of my inventories, but I just wasn't willing to see my part; it was all his fault. My sponsor and I decided that another inventory would be beneficial. I put the man's name at the top of my new resentment list. Every time I read his name out loud, I became filled with such rage that nothing else mattered.

One day my sponsor very kindly said, "Bill, why don't you consider that you may owe the man an amends?" I looked at him and did what I've been taught to do: I bit my tongue, nodded my head and said OK.

A week or so later, my wife and I were having a conversation. This man who had been the cause of many a fight between my wife and I came up in our discussion. The old rage began to take hold, and then I remembered my sponsor's words: "Bill, maybe you owe this guy an amends."

I was willing only to consider that maybe, just maybe, I owed this guy an amends. I felt just an ounce of willingness to consider it. As our conversation continued, I asked my wife a question. I can't remember the exact question, but I remember the answer like it was yesterday.

She stopped and looked at me and said, "Bill, during that time when you were drinking I had no one to turn to, no one to talk to. All I wanted to do was die, and there was one person who made me feel a little bit of happiness, who made life not so painful."

In that moment, I expected to be filled with rage. But surprisingly, I was filled with gratitude instead. I knew that at a time when I was causing great pain in my wife's life, at least she was able to get a bit of happiness. Not only did I begin to be grateful that my wife had found some happiness during that time, I now even had a sense of gratitude for this man. He had given my wife some happiness when I wasn't able to, when all I was worried about was my next drink. I knew right then that I owed this man an amends.

I tell this story not to impress you with my ability to forgive because honestly, if it had been up to me I would have killed the guy. I tell this story to share with you the ability of this program to work miracles in our lives if we just take the action and have a willingness to say, "OK, just maybe." Nothing more is required.

In my experience, I don't get the miracle and then take the action. I take the action and then the miracles happen. Many times, what AA suggests that I do doesn't look like the answer. But I have found that any action that AA has asked me to take has always ended with a result much better than I could have ever imagined.

Bill B.
Tahlequah, Oklahoma

The Medicine My Heart Needed
August 2022

What happens when I don't owe an amend because I haven't wronged the other person? They were the one who wronged me. How do I forgive?

In AA, when I get hurt I can talk to my sponsor and my sober sisters to feel better. They know me and direct me accordingly. I will usually write about it and then talk about it some more, and then pray. I take actions so my character defects don't act out. I can take things too far and then my side of the street gets muddy. I hate having to make amends because I couldn't keep my mouth shut.

I've learned to do the work first, pause, pray and do the Steps, so when I approach someone to make an amend, I'm coming from a spiritual place. It can be exhausting.

Not long ago, I had a very tricky situation come up in AA. I was at my home group, and I looked up to see the man who had raped me in the last days of my drinking. He was a newcomer. I was stunned. I immediately went over to a woman and asked her to be my safe person. We went to a safe place, and I told her what had happened.

God was working in my life, because she told me the very same thing had happened to her. She had the experience, strength and hope that I needed right then. What are the odds of that happening? I didn't know this woman all that well and I don't know why I made her my safe person other than there must have been a power greater than myself guiding me. After talking to her, I gathered some of my sober sisters and we went over to one of their homes nearby. I was not alone.

The next few days, I prayed a lot. I talked to my sponsor and we came up with a solution that felt safe, but ultimately she said it was my decision. I'm not going to get into what happened or why this was the best course of action. You will just have to believe me when I say this was a solution that was signed off on by more than just me.

I finally decided that he needed AA and that I could afford him the same chance at sobriety I had. He could also have anonymity. I allowed him to have my home group. I go to a lot of meetings, so dropping this one right now and embracing a different meeting as my home group was something I could do. It was a hard pill to swallow. I felt like he had taken so much from me already. But AA had been there for me at my bottom, and something in me said AA needed to be there for him now. I walked away. I neither accepted nor rejected him. I just allowed him to find his path without me in it.

Forgiveness is hard. It's the ultimate in letting go. Walking away without a word to him was one of the most spiritual things I feel I've ever done. I forgave him and I didn't do anything that involved him. The power of that altered everything in me. I don't think about him anymore. He no longer comes up on Fourth Steps. I don't owe him an amend; I don't need him to make amends to me. That's between him and his sponsor and his Higher Power. I have given all I have to give.

The Ninth Step is about making things right. I don't need him to make things right. I made them right. Forgiveness has been the medicine my heart needed to move toward health, happiness and love. I now get the opportunity to use this experience to help other women let go, forgive and live their lives sober, happy, joyous and free. AA gave me ... me.

Valerie T.
San Diego, California

Return to Sender

September 2023

After I'd been in the program for about three months, I started getting into the Steps, slowly. I kept hearing that the Fourth Step was really scary. But when I got to that Step, I thought all the people who said it was scary were nuts.

Writing about all the people that I was upset with, man, that was easy. However, looking at my part in these conflicts was not as easy. But I kept at it. I did the Fourth Step in the way my sponsor "suggested" and soon had a four-column inventory, just like the Big Book talked about. Being a rebel, I didn't write it down by hand. I typed it out. Then I hit print and had it in black and white in front of me.

The biggest resentment I had was toward my father, who had certainly done more harm to me than I had to him. Even after I did my Fifth Step, I still had a major resentment toward my father. I could be sitting in a meeting and someone would be talking about his or her dad and I would get mad. They didn't even have to be talking about problems with fathers, it could be about the good times they were having with them now in sobriety and I'd be mad as a wet hen.

At one point I was told to try the "Page 552 trick," which refers to the story "Freedom From Bondage" in the Fourth Edition of the Big Book, which mentions praying for the person that you have the resentment against. You pray that they have all the good things you want in life. Do this for two weeks and by the time you're finished you will find you mean it.

Well, I did this for a full month every morning, and at the end I still sat in meetings getting angry when someone would talk about his or her father.

By three years in the program, I was on my third sponsor. The first two had both gone back out. "Isn't it time you did something about the resentment and the amends for your father?" my new sponsor said.

I reluctantly agreed to write to my father. So I typed up the letter and emailed it to my sponsor, asking for his opinion on what I had written. He responded by removing this and adding that. After sending the email back and forth a number of times, we came to an agreement. We hit a meeting after that and went to a local burger shop to talk it over. I read the letter again and we agreed it was ready to be sent.

Now, the Big Book talks about being willing, and I was still not really willing to send that letter. So when my sponsor said, "Send it," I handed him the letter, an envelope and a $1 bill to buy a stamp. "I'm not going to send it," I said. He chuckled as he took the letter from me and said, "Good enough."

That meeting with my sponsor was on a Saturday. When I returned home from work the following Thursday, I checked the mailbox and the letter was in it. On it was written: "Return to sender."

I looked at the envelope in shock. I pulled out my cell phone and called my sponsor. I asked him to guess what was in the mail. He guessed it was a letter from my dad. Nope. I told him it was the very same letter we had sent. It was back. We talked about what that meant.

Since the day I got home and found the letter in my mailbox, my resentment is gone. I did my part. It's not up to me how my dad accepts or rejects my attempt to make things right. It's up to me to make the effort. That isn't to say that he and I are on speaking terms today, but I can share this story or hear others talk about their fathers without getting upset now.

About two years after all this happened, my sister contacted me saying that if I wanted to talk to our dad I had better hurry because his health was failing. "The last time I sent him a letter it came back unopened," I told her, and she thought that over. "Don't try to contact him," she said. "He has not changed."

I spoke with my sponsor at the time and he asked how long had it been since I had thought about my dad. It was hard to answer that question, as the resentment was gone.

Joseph S.
Reno, Nevada

Under the Banyan Tree
August 2013

When I wrote my first Eighth Step list, I had no trouble putting my mother at the top. In my Fourth Step, I had already itemized what I had stolen from her (money, jewelry, wedding silver). I knew what came next.

Admitting guilt has always been difficult for me. Lying came easily. I think my mother's legendary temper played a part in this. I grew up with her raging over even minor infractions. Frequently, as she said herself, she would completely come unglued. I felt that I needed to evade guilt at all costs. I had no doubt, after telling her the truth, that she would come completely unglued.

I put her name on the list, though not out of courage. I knew that I would never have to admit anything to her. She died before I got sober. I expected my sponsor to say to move on, but he didn't. Instead, he told me how alcoholics have been making amends to dead parents since the very beginning of AA.

He had me write a letter to my mother, being very specific about what I had stolen. I gave it to him to read over. He asked me to take out the references to my mother's temper and to rewrite the letter on something nicer than cheap notebook paper. He told me to seal it in an envelope and mail it. It seemed absurd to use a stamp, since the envelope was addressed to "Mom," but he said to do it anyway.

The next week, we met at a diner to talk about what came next: forgiveness. I didn't think my mother was any more likely to forgive me dead than alive. He wasn't talking about her forgiving me, however, but me forgiving her. I didn't think this was something I could do. He said that I had only begun to make my amends. He suggested that I go back to my hometown to leave flowers at my mother's grave. I made the trip, knowing that she had not been buried beside her parents. Her brother had not allowed it. Seeing her surrounded by strangers made me feel sorry for her, something new.

Next, I contacted my mother's beloved aunt, who had always given my mother love and encouragement. My mother frequently mentioned how grateful she was. My aunt burst into tears. She had felt guilty that she hadn't done enough. She then told me stories about my mother as a little girl, who sounded nothing like the woman I knew. She sent me a small album of fading photos of my parents' wedding. I hadn't realized how much my mother once looked like a young Katherine Hepburn. In one photo, she is flashing a dazzling, confident smile. I clearly didn't know this young woman.

I got back into contact with my siblings. I had virtually no relationship with either of them. I had moved away when they were barely out of grade school. I now attempted to be their older brother, something my mother would have wanted. To my surprise, my siblings responded. I ended up doing for them what my mother's aunt had done for me—fill in gaps in the past.

I was in the seventh grade when my parents divorced. My father moved away and remarried. My mother had to go to work to support us. In 1970, her options were very limited. We went on food stamps. She lost whatever control over her drinking that she once had. She went out every night and frequently did not come home at all. I would wake up some mornings to find strange men in the house. I think my moving away after high school scared her. She quickly remarried. She still drank heavily, but now at home. My siblings grew up with an angry stepfather, but it wasn't the reign of terror that I had known.

My siblings often didn't recognize the mother I described. I couldn't chalk this up simply to the gap in age between us. Their impressions frequently differed from each other. This opened my eyes to a particular kind of self-centeredness. Other people didn't necessarily experience the world as I did. I also realized that I had to make an amend to them.

On the night my mother died, I rushed back to her house and went directly to the basement, hoping to save old family photos from an inevitable purge. I found a box stuffed with scrapbooks and albums. I put it in the trunk of my car. I didn't tell my stepfather or my siblings what I had done. Old habits die hard, especially with "noble" motives.

I also told my siblings that I grew up feeling that our mother didn't care about me. They asked if this was why I vanished from their lives after high school. In those years, I kept contact with my mother to a minimum. I wouldn't answer her calls or return her messages. This went on for years. I now understand that I was inflicting a new kind of harm, what a wise member of my home group calls "causing suspicion." This is when a child's neglect makes a parent wonder if something bad has happened. I caused my mother to worry all the time. Had there been an accident? Was I in the hospital? Was I even alive? How do I know that she worried about me? In my third year, I finally opened the box that I had taken. My mother kept a journal of sorts. She wrote down just how much she had worried about me.

I had one especially resilient resentment against my mother. On days when she drank at home, she liked to crank up her Hawaiian records and dance the hula for the neighbors. I felt humiliated and was teased relentlessly. My sponsor and I talked about this. I mentioned that my mother had lived briefly in Hawaii as a teenager. She considered this to be one of the happiest periods of her life. She loved Hawaiian culture and became an accomplished hula dancer. Before my parents married, she set up a small hula school in our hometown, one of the first of its kind on the mainland. I heard these stories directly from her, usually when her drinking turned weepy. I went to the hotel where my parents honeymooned and sat outside, nursing a pineapple juice. I realized that I had acquired my mother's love of Hawaii, the first place where I finally felt somewhat comfortable in my skin. I wondered if it did something similar for her. After all this, I wish I could say that I had finally forgiven my mother.

In year seven, I started experiencing can't-get-out-of-bed depression. I turned to therapy, and my mother kept coming up over and over. My therapist seemed impressed by my amends. I didn't understand why. It had accomplished nothing. I continued to go to meetings and have service commitments, but nothing seemed to bring any relief. I told myself not to drink, no matter what, but I had no hope that anything would ever change.

Then, one day, everything changed. I made another trip to Hawaii, this time to attend an AA convention. One night, I went back to the hotel where my parents had honeymooned. The hotel is built around an enormous old banyan tree with a dense canopy of leafy branches. I ordered my pineapple juice. The waves crashed on the beach. A man played the ukulele. An old woman, her cloud of silver hair sitting on her shoulders like a shawl, sang Hawaiian songs that seemed familiar; they were ones my mother used to sing. I heard a burst of laughter from behind me. I watched a waitress take a picture of a young couple seated at a nearby table. I heard the young man, already bald, say that they were on their honeymoon. His beautiful bride had an enormous yellow hibiscus flower in her hair.

A memory hit me upside the head. I already had the photo the waitress just snapped, only it was faded and black-and-white. I came across it in that box that I had swiped from my mother's basement. In that old photo, there's a banyan tree, probably this one. My parents are the happy couple on their honeymoon. My father is already bald, and my mother has a big flower in her hair. They look so happy. Their future must have looked so bright to her. She could not have imagined what alcoholism would do to her dreams, her marriage, her children.

I suddenly felt overwhelmed by compassion for her. She was just like other women sitting around me in AA meetings, the ones who had loved and helped me countless times. The only difference was this: she had not gotten the gift of sobriety. All the anger and resentment vanished then and there. That was more than 10 years ago and it has not come back.

I don't sugarcoat my childhood. My mother may have done the best she could, but she did a lousy job. Still, I forgive her everything. It took finding compassion for her to do that. When I wrote that first letter, I had no idea how many years and different ways this amend would take. Fortunately, I kept trying, even though my efforts seemed to fail. Now, I think my "failures" actually prepared me for that moment under the banyan tree for the spiritual awakening about my mother.

Anonymous

STEP NINE

Made direct amends to such people wherever possible,
except when to do so would injure them or others.

————— ♦ —————

A *daughter persists in her amends for years—until her father
finally opens up his heart to her and the son he has never
seen. An AA makes an amends to his brother for something
he did while in a blackout, only to discover that his brother has
three years in the program and is making an amends to him. The
stories in this chapter, among the most moving in* Our Twelve
Steps, *truly capture the spirit of AAs taking responsibility, as Bill
W. writes in our book* Twelve Steps and Twelve Traditions, *"... for
their past acts, and for ... the well-being of others at the same time."
More than "apologies," our Ninth Step amends can provide us with
a newfound sense of self-confidence and a deepened intimacy with
those we love.*

What Matters Most

September 2021

My dad and I had a rocky relationship while I was drinking. He kicked me out and had very little to do with me near the end. But he did pick me up from detox and drive me to a rehab.

While I was in rehab, my younger brother went into hospice care at home. The rehab people gave me a pass to be with my family and my dad let me come and stay a few days until my brother passed. After he passed, I returned to rehab. My dad never talked to me again. I think my brother's passing made him terrified to have me in his life. He never knew when I was going to relapse and die.

At about a year and a half sober, I tried to make amends to my dad. He told me to lose his number and that he didn't want people like me in his life. At three years sober, I tried to make amends again and sent him a check. He sent it back. Soon after that, I reached out to let him know I was pregnant. During my pregnancy I sent him a card every month. He never wrote back. The moment my son was born, I sent him a digital photo announcing his birth.

That was the first time he texted me back. Something had shifted. He even helped me navigate some aspects of my son's care, as my son has special needs and so did my brother. We did all that communication by text. He has never met my son.

I called my dad and left a voicemail the day after my son's heart stopped for 35 minutes in the operating room. After the surgery, my son was in the intensive care unit in critical condition. My dad, who was out of the country at the time, texted me back, but didn't come to see my son.

I have continued to write to him and to send him photos of his grandson. I sent him gifts on holidays and wrote cards to him, one from from my son and one from me. I invited him to his grandson's birthday. He didn't come to the birthday, but he sent gifts worth hundreds of dollars. That's how he shows his love.

Over the years, we have begun to text more. We even have something like normal conversations through texts. But he won't answer my calls.

Then the other night something changed. He sent me a text in which he asked to see my son. We made plans to meet. My son is 18 months old, and he will meet his grandfather for the first time this week. I will see my dad for the first time in more than four years.

I write all this to let you know that sobriety works. Sometimes the results of our efforts to make amends take years. Sometimes they come after a lot of painful rejection. Making amends takes consistency, direction from a sponsor and God's grace. God's timing is often mysterious, but it's perfect.

In some ways, I'm glad that it has taken so long to rebuild a relationship with my dad, because over that time I have become a person that I'm proud for him to see. I've had 5 years to learn how to be a good daughter and a good example. I pray that he will see that. But this meeting with him is not about me. I'm going to step aside and allow my son to meet his grandpa. I will let them just have that. What matters most to me is that my son will have another family member to love him.

Kristin S.
Fullerton, California

A Tough Amend
September 2021

I recently turned 60, and one month later I reached my 32nd AA anniversary. Although my recovery has been quite stable, about a month ago I received some very bad news in an email from my cousin who lives on Long Island in New York.

A man I had known since boyhood had died. I cried when I read about his death. His name was Leon. I had made amends to him when I was just a few years sober. The memory of him made me think about the worst day of my life.

I was just 6 years old when I first met Leon. My mom and dad had gotten a divorce when I was 2. One evening, my mom told me that she was going on a date. She said that our next-door neighbor was going to babysit me while she was out. "If a man arrives while I'm getting ready," she told me, "just let him in."

When the doorbell rang, I was sitting by the TV and I jumped up to answer the door. A man was standing there. "My name is Leon," he said. He asked whether my mom was available. I said she was getting ready, and I asked if he was going to be my new daddy.

Leon was a widower, I later found out. His wife had died two years earlier. Their date that night must have been successful, because a year later Leon and my mother were married. They were together for eight years. During that time, I became a full-blown alcoholic. When I found out they were getting a divorce, I was full of alcoholic rage.

One night, I came home very late and totally drunk. Leon was there as I stumbled in. I started yelling at him. He refused to talk to me while I was drunk and told me to go to my room to sleep it off. I stormed off in a rage. When I got to my room, I grabbed a hunting knife from my closet and stormed back to confront Leon. Again he refused to talk to me, and he turned his back. I was so drunk that I was not in my right mind. I raised the knife and stabbed him in the back. As I pulled the knife out, he gave out a horrible scream of pain, which is a sound I will never forget.

Instead of falling to the floor dead, Leon turned around and started punching me. One punch landed on my face and I fell to the floor where I hit my head on something and passed out. When I came to, a policeman was standing above me. I had been handcuffed and my legs were restrained.

Leon was at my trial in juvenile court. When the trial was over, I was convicted of attempted murder. As the judge read his ruling, he informed me that arrangements had been made for me to live with my biological father in Japan. In less than a week, I was on an airplane.

Over the next 13 years, my alcoholism went from bad to worse. At 28 years old, I stumbled drunk into my first AA meeting. Through the grace of God and the program of AA, I have not had a drink since that first meeting.

After several years sober, I applied to law school and was accepted. Several months before moving to begin law school, my sponsor told me that before I went to school, I should travel back to New York to make amends to Leon. I had made many amends up to that point, but not to Leon.

A month later I was on an airplane headed for New York. When I arrived, I rented a car and drove to Leon's place of business. I got there about 11:00 A.M. I sat in the car frozen with fear. I just could not go in. Instead, I headed for a noon AA meeting in town. As I walked in, the secretary came over to me and asked if I was a newcomer. I said that I was not a newcomer and that I was traveling from California. The secretary asked if I would like to chair the meeting. I said yes.

I told my story and admitted to the group why I was there. I explained that I had so far failed to make the amends. After the meeting, an elderly couple thanked me for speaking. The man said he and his wife would be happy to go back with me to Leon's business to give me moral support in making my amends.

We drove our cars over to Leon's business. When we got out of our cars, they both told me they would wait for me. With the couple's encouragement, I walked in the front door. I told the secretary my name and that I would like to speak to Leon if I could. She went into his office.

I stood frozen in fear. When the office door opened, I thought I was going to have a heart attack. I had not seen Leon for 18 years. Suddenly, he appeared in the doorway. He looked me over and then walked over and wrapped his arms around me, giving me a big bear hug. I burst into tears and it seemed like I could not stop. And then we walked into his office where we sat down, and I started to speak. We spoke for almost two hours. Years of baggage seemed to fall off of me.

When I left his office, I felt relief that's hard to describe. The AA couple had waited outside all that time. I told them what had happened and thanked them, and we parted company.

In the following years, I stayed in touch with Leon. The redemption I received gave new meaning to my AA program, which has stood the test of time. I'm so grateful for the blessings I received through this program. I now have a wonderful memory when I think of Leon.

Bob K.
Benicia, California

If It Ain't Nailed Down
March 2013

While my drinking career only spanned five years, my alcoholic behavior had been such that I had a really long list of people to whom I owed amends. At first I felt really hopeless about it. I thought I'd made such a mess of my life that it couldn't possibly be fixed. Still, I began the process of making those amends, starting with my family first and then working through my list. Each amend I made gave me a little more hope that perhaps my life could change.

My sponsor helped me sort through which of the amends I needed to make directly, and which ones would be harmful to others. She also steered me away from making amends for things when she didn't think I'd done anything wrong. One that she claimed I didn't need to make was to the adolescent treatment center in which I'd found sobriety. I felt horribly guilty because when I left, I took a lot of things from the facility. I stole small things, like books, but bigger things too, like a lamp and a comforter, and pretty much anything that I liked that wasn't nailed down. Besides, the facility was closing, and I thought it was better to take the stuff for someone who could use it (me!) than to leave it for the parent corporation to reallocate to other facilities. A disgruntled employee had actually helped me load the goods into my car.

My sponsor reasoned that if the facility was closing at the time of my departure, it wasn't really stealing. I felt guilty, though, because the facility ended up reopening a few months later. My sponsor kept telling me that I needed to just let this one go, but it didn't feel right. I was certainly living my life differently, but despite my sponsor's view of the situation, I couldn't just let it go. I finally told her that I was going to make amends anyway, and I called the facility to ask what their needs were. I wasn't financially in a position to make a huge monetary amend, but I figured I could start by buying them some bedding or donating some clothes for the residents who sometimes arrive with only the clothes on their backs.

The woman who answered the phone had worked there when I was a resident and was delighted to hear from me. She was happy to hear that I was still sober and doing well. I told her why I was calling—what I had done years before and what I wanted to do about it. She told me that they didn't need goods, but they did need volunteers. It seemed that a small group of local AA members that had been bringing meetings into the center had stopped coming, and since the facility was a lockdown, that meant the residents no longer got to go to any AA meetings at all. She asked me if I'd be willing to talk to my AA friends and bring in regular meetings.

At first, this seemed like too much of a request. I lived almost two hours away. And while I was connected to AA in my local community, I didn't know many people in the district where the treatment center was located. But I talked to some of my local connections, particularly other young people, and found several members who really wanted to do this. So I committed to doing it with them, and we started a Saturday night meeting in the facility.

Sometimes we'd go early and have dinner with the residents, and we'd almost always stay after and hang out. It was a great commitment and a wonderful way for me to make a living amend. I kept this commitment until I moved out of the area.

The best part of making this amend is that now, when I think of the facility, I don't feel guilty at all. I remember the kids and the meetings and the service—not the stolen goods in my trunk.

Karen P.
Franklin, New Hampshire

Swimming With Mom
February 2017

I sat across from my sponsor, Ginny, at a diner on 23rd Street and 9th Avenue in New York City. I recited my Eighth Step list of people who I had harmed and to whom I needed to make amends.

We went through the list one by one. As I said, "My mom," tears welled up in my eyes. I tried to stop, but one tear escaped down my cheek. I quickly brushed it away. Ginny never said a word. "How can I ever make amends to her?" I asked. "She's dead."

Ginny told me to write a letter and go to her grave and read it out loud to her. So I went to New Jersey and said some things out loud to her at her grave. My sister was with me. We both cried, but something did not feel right. I did not feel Mom's presence there.

I thought back to times where I really remembered being with her. Then I recalled a time when I was swimming with her in Florida. She wasn't sick yet back then, or at least we hadn't yet realized that she was. Neither did we know how little time we had left with her.

In my memory, I saw her big blue eyes and long wet blond hair. I saw her swimming, her sidestroke. I remembered it was dusk and the water was warm as bath water. It was so peaceful. I didn't know it would be the last time I would swim with my mom before she passed.

We had been swimming at the beach near Balboa Street in Hollywood, Florida, which was near what had once been our home. We lived there when my children were very young—when I was very young. I decided that I'd return to the beach at Balboa Street to make my amends.

So I flew to Ft. Lauderdale. I met up with Troy, a friend I'd known in New York who was now living in Florida. I went to an AA meeting he recommended. I told him I had come there to make my amends to Mom. I went to various other meetings. I went to the beach and explored where I had lived before. It seemed like a lifetime ago. The place was so different now. And I was different. I was sober. I got so busy while I was there that I lost track of time. One night, I had dinner with Troy and a bunch of friends from AA. "Have you made your amends?" he asked. I told him I hadn't yet.

Early the following morning, I headed for Hollywood Beach. I felt Mom's presence on the drive over Dania Beach Boulevard, which we had driven so many times. I felt her presence so strongly that I looked over at the car's passenger seat to see if she was there. I remembered that when we'd driven down that road, it was at that certain time of year when the crabs would cross the road. They were all over. Try as we might to avoid them, we'd hear the "crunch" as we drove over a few of them. I laughed and cried at the memory.

This had been "our beach." Now there was a big condominium complex that overlooked what was once a beautiful beach. I remembered watching people fly kites there and the scuba divers going diving. I remembered Mom trying to fly a kite with my kids. It was just beach and ocean then. Now it was all brick and mortar. The house we lived in was gone, swallowed by the advancing ocean. It was drizzling that morning and I was alone. It was just the ocean and me. Or was it?

I felt my mom was somehow with me there as I walked into the waves. They were soft and warm. I cried and told Mom how sorry I was for getting drunk and running in front of a car on that street (something I didn't remember at the time). I told her how sorry I was for leaving my children with her so I could go get drunk and then hitch a ride to buy drugs. I told her I was also grateful that she had always been there for me, during all the rehabs and psychiatric ward stays (and there were many). She even came to California to take care of my children when I was in these places. God blessed me with a mother who loved me drunk and sober and loved my children more than her own.

I cried into the waves. I screamed as loud as I wanted into the sound of the ocean until it was all I could hear. I walked through the waves back to shore and wrote a letter to her. Then I walked back out into the surf, as deep as I could go. I released the letter to the ocean. I watched it float away, pulled into the ocean waves.

She never gave up on me. And she never stopped loving me. She was, and will always be, my best friend.

Romee D.
New York, New York

The Road From Reno
September 2014

As the plane took off my father asked, "Is it going to bother you if I use these two free drink coupons on this flight?" He wasn't going to drink them, but they were free and he was a frugal man. I was just about two years sober and the last thing he wanted to do was to put my sobriety at risk. At my first AA birthday he had asked my sponsor, "How much do I owe you?" That was the only way he knew how to say thank you. We are not wealthy by any means, and I had lived on my own for more than 20 years, but he was grateful for what AA had done for me and my family.

This trip was part of the process of making amends to my parents. My mother had asked me if I'd help drive a car back from Reno, Nevada. She had purchased it from her brother's estate. I said yes, of course. I had my wife's OK to go; she knew I needed to do it (thank God for Al-Anon).

In Reno everything happens around the casino. My uncle's wife was part of a group of older ladies who ate breakfast in the casino, went back for lunch, and then, after a nap, went back for dinner to play a bit of keno. So I had to spend quite a bit of time in the casino. To my surprise, I never had a thought of drinking.

I escaped the temptations of the "Biggest Little City in the World," and we drove back to our hometown of Memphis, Tennessee in Mom's new car. It was a long trip, and I drove the biggest part of it. It was the least I could do for my parents; after all, they had rescued me time and time again. I even had them smuggling in food on the weekend while I was in the penal farm, or as I lovingly called it, the Shelby County Country Club, where I did a one to three-year sentence for crimes related to my drinking. In other words, I owed them a lot more than I could ever pay back by driving from Reno to Memphis.

My father and I had had those frank and honest talks about what I had done and about how I could make it right. We both had admitted our faults, and I had done what was necessary to clean my side of the street. Of course, me staying sober was the biggest part as far as he was concerned. I was very grateful to have been able to get that one under my belt.

As we were driving back from Reno, Dad and I were in the front seat and Mom was in the back seat. Everything was just rolling along; life was good. I had talked to my wife and son back home and they were eagerly anticipating my return, all as a result of the new lease on life AA had given me. As the conversation in the front seat turned to the past, I thought maybe this was the right time to have that frank and honest talk with Mom about all of my faults and past misdeeds— to clear the air, so to speak. It seemed to be the perfect opportunity to make "direct amends" to her, so I launched into some of the details of my past transgressions, and said that if I could, I'd go back and redo things. I added how much I regretted doing those things.

Then I looked into the mirror, and I saw the look in her eyes. I knew immediately that these things I was bringing up caused her to remember the dark days of the decades before I entered AA. I could see the pain that I was putting her through as she remembered those times when she didn't know if her baby was dead or alive. Not to mention the time when her youngest son was sentenced to the state penitentiary for the crimes he had committed while under the influence. And did I need to make her remember the time when she brought my two children from my first marriage to visit me at Christmas, in a gymnasium inside that penitentiary? Those were just a handful of the situations I had forced her to endure. I knew immediately I had no right to bring up those painful memories. Trying to right the wrongs of my past, I was causing her more pain.

Thank God for good sponsorship, because Jack and I had discussed the Ninth Step and what it says about making "direct amends" to people, "except when to do so would injure them or others." The rule of thumb is: hard on us, easy on others. I don't have the right to hurt those people any more, and I have to bear the burden on my own two shoulders.

With Mom I have continued to make those amends by doing whatever I could to be of service to her. For many years, I called her every day and would go by whenever she needed something, or just whenever I thought I could help in any way—even when she didn't ask. Before my father died a few years ago, I was able to help Mom take care of him and make the arrangement for his funeral, like a good son should. And thanks to making amends to him, I was "square" with him and could say goodbye without any regrets.

Three years later, when my mom got sick, I was there for her too. The result of that was that she decided she didn't have to live alone. Finally, she consented to me building a wing for her on the back of my house and getting her out of the old neighborhood. I don't have the right to rob her of her independence to satisfy my need to know she is taken care of. Her apartment is totally self-contained, except for the laundry room, which we share. Mom has her own entry to a garden area and flowerbed, so she can do the gardening she loves so much. Her place has many windows, so she can have plenty of light to paint.

Some folks use the term making "living amends" when you can't have one of those frank and honest talks. But really, isn't changing the way we do things the true spirit of making direct amends? I'll never be able to undo my past, but I don't have to continue to be haunted by it if I just follow the path that has been laid out for me by those who trudged the road before me.

Don A.
Germantown, Tennessee

To Love a Dad
June 2023

I'm not a "one-chip wonder." I tried a while to get the program. It took a year of near-daily AA meetings, my fifth DWI conviction, a 28-day treatment center and a half dozen beginner chips for me to begin my sober life. Only then did I become serious about staying sober and become willing to work the Steps.

I worked my first five Steps in treatment and exited with a plan to work Steps Six through Nine. My first sponsor taught me how to work the Tenth, Eleventh and Twelfth Steps on a daily basis and I have started my day with my "spiritual breakfast" every day of my sobriety.

It's easy for me to see now that much of my difficulty in getting sober was my inability to see myself as an alcoholic. When I was 5 years old, one evening at dusk my father and I were out driving. I was in the passenger seat. Suddenly, his right arm shot across my face and he pointed out the window and yelled, "That's an alcoholic!" He said it with all the disgust and contempt one man can have for another. I looked out and saw a man in a raincoat lying in the gutter under an overpass with his arm extended while holding a brown bag with the neck of a bottle sticking out of it. That image was still my definition of an alcoholic when I walked into the rooms of AA at age 43.

As an adult, I wore a suit and tie to work and was a highly paid middle manager of the business development department at the most prestigious company in our city. As I saw it, there was no way I could be like that man I had seen in the gutter. But I knew something was wrong. It took a year of AA meetings and the study of AA literature for me to see myself and to change my definition of an alcoholic. "The Doctor's Opinion" in the Big Book was particularly significant. Dr. Silkworth observed that the alcoholic has an obsession of the mind that creates an urge to drink, along with a craving to drink more. With that definition, I easily saw myself in my actions and motivations for 23 years of my life.

Like many sons, I had a difficult relationship with my father. I desperately wanted his approval and seemingly never could get it. I was a pretty good athlete, a basketball "star" in high school and college. My father didn't come to a single high school game and saw only one of my college games. Once, when I sank eight of 10 shots from the foul line, my father asked me how I could miss two shots from only 15 feet with no one guarding me.

Over time, I built up a lot of resentments against him because he often made me feel less-than. I couldn't see that in his way he was probably just trying to push me to be the best that I could be.

When I got sober, my father was a daily drinker. At age 74, his life was always the same, like the film, "Ground Hog Day." In late morning he traveled six city blocks to visit and argue with his buddies at a local tavern and get drunk on eight-ounce draft beer. After going home and sleeping that off, he repeated the process in mid-afternoon and did it once again in the evening. He'd get up the next day and do it all again.

This is the same man who was a short-order cook when I was born. He saved his money and eventually opened his own diner, where he worked 12-hour days, six days a week, 50 weeks a year, year after year, with the main objective of putting me and my two sisters through college.

At two months sober, I was able to arrange a business trip from my home in North Carolina to upstate New York, with an opportunity to visit my parents. Before I left, I went to my daily AA meeting in the late afternoon. When the chairperson asked for a topic, I spouted off about my intent to go on this trip and get my father sober. It turned out to be quite a meeting. At one point, my sponsor said, "Can't get yourself sober, but now you're going to pester that poor man." Later in the meeting, a lady with a lot of sobriety said, "I'll bet you have some amends to make to that man."

After the meeting, my sponsor took me aside. "Do you really want him to get sober?" he asked. I said I did. He then asked, "Are you willing to pray that he experience the depth of pain required to get someone to walk into our rooms?" I said I thought I couldn't do that. "Then go there and love him," he told me. When I told my sponsor I didn't know how to do that, he said, "Then pray that you find out how."

I flew to the small airport in Binghamton, New York, where my father picked me up. His car was parked in the one-way, no-parking area, pointing the wrong way, and he was being watched by three policemen. My father's battered car had so many dents that some of them had straightened out others. I told him I would drive the car out of there and, incredibly, the police let us go.

We drove to the home where I grew up. My father knew that I had recently gone to treatment, but as we sat down at the kitchen table, he went to the refrigerator, got a beer and put it in front of me. I didn't get angry. I just said, "No, thanks. I'm trying to not drink".

We started talking and I was praying to learn how to love him. All of a sudden it came to me: I was there to do my Ninth Step with him and now I knew how to make my amends. Until that moment I had never seen that he had always been there for me, even when I didn't want him to be there. And worse than that, I had taken all of his support and guidance for granted and never thanked him for any of it. Through his labors, he had put me through five years of college at one of the most expensive universities in our country. He supported me and my wife when we had no money because she and I married in college. And even after I graduated, he bailed me out of more situations that I can remember.

Now, with one day left of my visit, I finally understood that in one way or another he was responsible for creating the opportunities for all of the successes I have enjoyed in my life. We sat down and I thanked him for everything that he had done for me.

After a moment, he said, "Richard, I want to stay with you all day tomorrow, and I won't drink." We spent the next day together. At dinner, I noticed that with no alcohol my father was very shaky. It was a Saturday, and we went to the evening mass at the church of my youth. Mass was sparsely attended and we sat in a pew by ourselves. As always, near the end of the mass, we stood, held hands and recited the Lord's Prayer. I was 45 and my dad was 74 but I felt like a little boy holding my hero's hand. For the first time since childhood, I was fully at peace with my dad. I felt real love for him. I felt like I was sitting on top of the world.

I finished my business trip and flew back home to North Carolina. Three weeks later, I received a phone call telling me that my father had passed away in his sleep. At his funeral, I cried and cried. Words will never be able to describe my gratitude to the AA people and program that guided me through my Ninth Step with my dad when I was just two months sober.

By God's grace, I've been sober for more than 32 years now. And like so many others, AA has given me an incredibly good life. I often wonder now if the reason my father never made it to AA was that he never had help in understanding the real definition of an alcoholic.

Dick H.
Winston-Salem, North Carolina

What a Ride
September 2018

I run a small roller coaster fan club and one year, our group planned a trip to California. One of the days of the trip was a free day, so since I hadn't seen my brother in several years, I called him and suggested we spend the day alone together at Disneyland.

That morning, my brother arrived at my hotel. We had a quick breakfast and walked the four blocks to the park. We rode so many memorable rides and enjoyed each other's company. While we were waiting to get on a ride, we decided to sit and chat for a while.

As we talked, I brought up the one thing he was still upset about regarding our lives back when we lived with our parents. I had once told my mother something about my brother that was highly personal. On a previous visit to California, I had made my amends to him regarding this, but it was still bugging me. I could see he was still edgy about it too.

My brother wanted to know why I had told my mother this information and why I would never admit to it in the past. As I sat there talking, a thought popped into my head: I could very well have been in a blackout at the time I told our mother this info! So I said this.

All of a sudden, my brother's eyes lit up. Now he understood that I wasn't lying all these years. I didn't remember it.

Afterward, my brother thanked me and then he turned the conversation to his actions. He spoke about how he wasn't there for me. He began to list the times that he had not been a good big brother. He then asked for my understanding.

"Wow," I said. "If I didn't know better, I'd swear you're doing a Ninth Step amends." He looked me in the eyes and said, "I am." Then he told me he had three years of sobriety. I had no idea.

Our conversation became a lot easier after that. We left Disneyland that day with both of our slates clean.

God always knows the right time for things and this moment couldn't have happened soon enough. My brother passed away less than a year later. What a wonderful blessing recovery is. I'm so glad we have this program that allows us to heal our lives.

Sam M.
Alexandria, Virginia

A Very Strange Amend
February 2017

Last night after making a direct amends with someone I had put off for four years, I got in a car accident at 55 mph. Thank goodness I was OK.

The police officer at the scene asked me if I would like to stay warm in his cop car. My first thought was, Hell no. However I said, "Yes, thank you." He took me over to his car, moved some equipment from the back so I could get in, and then said, "If you need anything, you'll have to knock, because it doesn't open from the inside."

I thought to myself, Oh yes, I am familiar with that. Your kind and mine go way back.

While I sat in the back of the cop car, I got a text from that friend of mine whom I just sat face-to-face with 30 minutes ago. I had been in her living room, owning up to my selfishness, and we were both sobbing healing tears together. Before I left her house I let her know that if there was anything at all that she remembered that we hadn't talked about that hurt her, to not hesitate to tell me. I wanted to know so I could make things right.

So here I was, sitting in the back of this cop car, getting a text from her asking me about lies I had told. She was asking me what the truth was. I looked up over the dashboard of the cop car. I contemplated this accident and thought, Am I willing to go to any lengths for freedom?

So I texted her back. I didn't change the subject. I didn't bring up the accident. I didn't use it as an excuse to shy away and make her feel sorry for me. I didn't lie. I told the truth. I owned up. I faced the reality of my past, sitting right here in the middle of my present, and answered her questions.

Soon my boyfriend arrived to get me and the police officer opened the car door. I thanked him for keeping me warm. I thought to myself, Look at this, I'm being let out of this cop car. What a story where I come from.

After I pay rent this month, I'll have just $40 in my checking account. I have no idea what's coming next. I don't have a car right now. But what I feel and know in my heart is this: Nothing, absolutely nothing, can touch the peace and serenity that is in me. Nothing can touch the Promises I get from being willing to do these Ninth Step amends. Not even a car accident and the loss of material things.

It's now 11 o'clock the following morning and I'm sitting at my kitchen table crying because I am so grateful God has brought me to this place. I'm sober. And today, I'm a good and honest friend. Funny how healing works.

Katie S.
West Bend, Wisconsin

STEP TEN

Continued to take personal inventory and when we were wrong
promptly admitted it.

———————— ♦ ————————

A personal inventory (done as soon as possible) can be used
in all walks of life—at home, at work, with friends—to right
wrongs and correct errors, with the twin goals of not letting
guilt or anger fester and improving our relationships with others. In "Summer of Love," Karen W. describes a moment she experienced years ago as a beginner, when she watched a meeting
chair publicly apologize to a homeless man for being unkind to
him after the man foraged for cookies at an AA refreshment table.
"That incident happened almost 25 years ago," she writes, "but the
memory of that amends ... has never left me." The stories in this
chapter show the importance of being able to heal our lives through
honesty and forthrightness, "day in and day out," as Bill W. writes
in Twelve Steps and Twelve Traditions, "in fair weather and foul."

Even If the Truth Hurts
October 2019

Years ago, when I was just a few months into my newfound sobriety, I was confronted with a situation that most parents have experienced. On this occasion, my eldest daughter had been caught up in the worst kind of trouble that a 9-year-old girl can engage in—lying.

Naturally, as a concerned father I was furious to hear that my precious daughter had been lying to me and her mother about her school work. It wasn't until I got a letter from her teacher and found missing assignments stashed in her backpack that I knew for sure that she had been dishonest with us for quite some time, even when we asked her if her studies were done.

I was devastated. My innocent, loving, caring daughter with whom I share a special day (my sobriety day is her birthday) had lied.

My wife and I were very upset and we wondered what else she might have been lying about. We wondered if this was only the tip of the iceberg. I wondered how this would affect my relationship with my daughter. These all were things I should have talked to my sponsor about, had I enough sense to call him. But I felt certain that I could handle it without his help.

So without consulting anyone, neither my wife nor my sponsor, I took it upon myself to "take care of it." And boy, did I ever.

While I drove my daughter to school the next day, I proceeded to criticize her actions and warned her of the severe consequences she would receive for lying. After an entire car ride of me spewing anger at her, I noticed that we were late to school by about 10 minutes because I couldn't stop myself from going on and on about how awful what she did was. My daughter, with her head down in shame, left my car humiliated. I thought, I won. She'll never do that again.

I watched her walk into the school and I saw through the vestibule glass that she had been stopped by the school secretary. My daughter was clearly getting an earful again, only this time from someone other than me.

Well, I wasn't having that. I parked my car, walked into the school, and there was my daughter getting told that she could not come late into the school without a note from her parents explaining her tardiness.

"No worries," I said. "We had a bit of car trouble." Without even thinking about what I was doing, I had lied in front of my daughter. She looked up at me with her big brown eyes and I sunk. In that moment, I wished the earth would just swallow me up. I left the school ashamed.

I went back home later and told my wife what had happened. She smiled and said perhaps I should apologize to my daughter. I also spoke with my sponsor, who laughed and pointed out that perhaps I should have asked for advice first, not after the damage was done. He added that the incident was something that I would never forget. I may have been right in being angry, he said. I may also have been right in talking to her, but I was horribly mistaken to shame her. It was the love of my wife and my daughter that led me back into the rooms of AA. My sponsor pointed out all the lies I spoke while I was drinking. He also pointed out to me that perhaps the reason I was so angered by Kylie's dishonesty was in part because it reminded me of myself.

I got off the phone and immediately apologized to my wife for the times I was dishonest to her. Then I picked up my daughter from school and apologized to her for my lie. We promised each other never to lie again, even if the truth hurts. She told me that she had figured out something about life. The truth may hurt for a short time, but a lie hurts all the time.

I learned a great deal from my daughter that day and a great deal about myself. That was one of the best days of my sobriety.

Kevin M.
Winchester, Virginia

Pause Button

October 2016

I recently went on a sober vacation in a beautiful paradise-like setting. And yet, despite the wonderful surroundings, I found myself in
the position of having to practice the Tenth Step not once, but twice.

First, I had to apologize to a woman whom I'd never even met before because I was quite rude to her almost as soon as I arrived. I was
talking with the trip organizer about the fact that I had been assigned
the wrong room. This woman joined the conversation. As we had no
idea who she was, I said in a voice just dripping with sarcasm, "And
you are?" She promptly answered that she was the organizer's wife.
She then stormed off, calling back to her husband that she would see
him later.

I gave her no thought in the moment. My focus was on getting the
right room because that trip was all about me. It was my vacation.

But as the day wore on, my behavior wore on me. I didn't like what
I saw or felt myself doing. I saw the woman alone that night waiting
for the meeting to begin. I took a deep breath and made my Tenth
Step move.

I reminded her who I was, which turned out to be unnecessary. She
remembered exactly who I was. I apologized to her for my earlier rude
behavior. Her whole face changed, as did her demeanor, and she said
that my apology meant a lot to her. In that moment, I could see that I
had really hurt her feelings. Who knew I had that much power over a
stranger? But words can wound both stranger and friend.

Thinking all was now well, I held out my hand. I said, "So, friends?"
To which she replied, after a long pause, "It's a start." That was all I
could ask for.

The second Tenth Step opportunity that I created occurred at
the airport on the way home. The trip was hot and hectic from the

start. By the time we got to our flight connection, everyone's nerves were frayed.

Two women were in front of me at the customs desk, but I interrupted to ask a brief question of the customs agent. Hey, it's all about me, right? The women took offense at my interruption. I nastily replied, "Oh, so what."

This time I immediately felt bad. Still, I kept walking. But wouldn't you know it, we met again on the line for our connecting flight. I apologized, they graciously accepted and we began talking like we were old friends.

For me, the Tenth Step is really two parts. First, I ask whether I was wrong. Back when I was drinking, the words, "when we were wrong promptly admitted it," were completely foreign to me. They might as well have been written in another language. My default when in the wrong was to lash out with angry words and place the blame anywhere but with me. It was a way I used to let off steam when under pressure. I realize now, in sobriety, there are better ways to let off steam.

Second, I admit I was wrong. When I was active, I was never wrong. In sobriety, I find I am indeed wrong sometimes, and it's not the end of the world as I know it. This amend can be tricky because I'm never sure how the person will react to an apology. Will they be gracious and forgiving like the women in the airport? Will they be unforgiving and cold? I've decided it doesn't really matter how the person reacts. I've done my part by apologizing. That's all I can do.

I can rationalize my way out of feeling the need for a Tenth Step action. It's easy to justify conduct that was hurtful, wrong, dishonest or inappropriate. But if I have to rationalize my behavior away, chances are good an apology is necessary.

I may try to justify my actions by saying I had good reason to do what I did. I may say he or she had it coming. But do my motives and reasons for what I did really matter when I know my actions have hurt someone? If I step on someone's toe and say I'm sorry, their toe still hurts and needs attention.

When I promptly admit I was wrong, I help myself feel better by not stewing in guilt or suffering the pain of delay. I prevent the wrong I've done from taking up space in my head and dragging me down.

In practicing Step Ten, I learn behavior that can prevent the need for future apologies. I begin to cultivate a pause button, so to speak, and allow for a pause between the thought and the action or words.

After seeing that woman's face change so much that day, I do believe there's magic in the Tenth Step—for everyone involved.

Dorothy G.
Staten Island, New York

Lie of Omission
October 2022

Talk of amends to others and institutions can find us in a "gray zone" where many in AA seem to think making amends is open to personal interpretation. The question then has to be asked: Where does one find themselves in the space between personal interpretation and moral loopholes?

I have been in many a meeting when someone, after hearing the above, will scream in their trolling twitter best, "There is no space for not taking the suggestions of this program!"

I had just over 18 months of sobriety when I kissed a woman who was not my girlfriend. The kiss felt like the many second sips I took while drinking: hollow, shame-filled and a step toward being morally numb. Immediately after I extricated myself from the situation, I called for help. I talked to my sponsor and other men I respect in the program. Their responses fell into two camps. The first said, "This is a program of rigorous honesty," and the second, "One law above all others: do no harm."

The questions that followed in my brain were: Do you fall into that category of those who are constitutionally incapable of being honest or do you want to hurt your girlfriend even more by telling on yourself? The answer to both of these questions was no.

These questions raised even more questions. Was I not going to tell her because I did not wish to hurt her or because my ego wanted a clean slate? In the case of the latter, it seemed to be self-serving, but it spoke to a question of motivation.

Setting my questions aside, it was clear to me that fear was completely ruling my thinking. I was afraid that my girlfriend would leave me if I told her what I had done. At the same time, I was afraid that not telling her would start the slippery slope of the white lies that used to lead me to drinking.

Does a lie of omission mean I'm not living the principles of the program? Does it mean I need to do another sex inventory? Am I a sexaholic? Did I just destroy this relationship, as I had done with so many in my past?

If at this point, you are confused or doubt your original stance on the subject, know that you are not alone. I felt the same way.

At the end of the day, I decided against telling my girlfriend. In the months that followed, our love for each other continued to grow and I stayed sober. I thought this whole incident was a lesson in living amends. I certainly did not do anything like that again. However, my Higher Power had other ideas.

About four months after the event, the woman I had kissed reached out via social media to my girlfriend and told her what had happened, stating that had she known we were dating she never would have done it.

When confronted with the message, I admitted to my girlfriend what I had done and I said I had didn't tell her about it because I did not want to hurt her, an excuse since the beginning of time with the value of a paper tiger. However, what happened after I admitted to it that night was a spiritual experience I will never forget.

My girlfriend and I did not speak for a week to allow us to cool off. I spent the week sleepless. My mind would wake me at 3:00 A.M. with feelings of self-loathing, depression and fear that she would dump me.

I wondered whether I could ever be in a relationship without destroying it. I went to meetings and tried to listen, but was so distracted that no pearls of wisdom sank in.

I knew that I did not want to be a philanderer or someone who betrays the trust of my partner. I prayed about it. I told myself that I was willing to go to any lengths to figure this out. I reached out to a therapist for the first time in my life. After five days, I got a text from my girlfriend asking me to meet her at a restaurant to talk. The place she asked to meet at was where we had one of our first dates.

Leading into the meeting, I again chatted with men I respected and my sponsor about what I should say. I was fully aware that it could be the end or that it could be a restart or it could be somewhere in between. What I hoped for was just the openness to accept whatever came. Both of us looked exhausted after a week of emotional turbulence and lack of sleep.

Did I want it all to go back to the way it was? No. Did I want her to forget it ever happened? No. Did she expect me to be a saint? No. Was I open to whatever happened? Yes.

What did happen was something so simple yet profound that I wish it to happen to everyone going through the amends process.

Throughout our conversation, we each had single tears drip from our eyes multiple times. The tears came when we talked honestly about how much we cared about each other, about how we didn't want our story to end and what the next steps might look like. There is still a lot of rebuilding of touch, trust, and transparency that needs to be done, but I am willing to do the work to make it better.

I hope to have more single-tear conversations.

Chris S.
Arlington, Virginia

Summer of Love

October 2013

One of the great things about getting sober in San Francisco is the wide range of meetings a newbie can choose from. My first year in sobriety, I would hop on a bus and go to a meeting in the Sunset district, walk to the Presidio for a women's meeting, or catch a ride with my sponsor and join the earlybirds at the 7 A.M. meeting in the Mission district.

One day I found myself in the meeting room of a Haight Ashbury clinic. The meeting was well attended, and somehow 40 or 50 people managed to jam themselves into a very small space filled with very uncomfortable folding chairs. The door to the meeting room opened right onto the corner of Haight and Ashbury. The neighborhood is noted for its colorful characters: hippies, street people, musicians, artists, tourists and drug users. A large coffeepot and a tray of cookies were set up next to the front door and the folding chairs were positioned facing the opposite wall. This gave the chairperson a clear view of the door and the comings and goings of the participants.

The folks in the meeting represented the diversity that the city is so famous for. A grandmother sat knitting in one corner, a tattooed teenager clutching his skateboard lounged in the front, and a Chinese businessman in his pinstriped suit sat next to me in the middle row. The chairperson was a middle-aged man who was fairly new to the program. His enthusiasm for AA was infectious. Before the meeting began, I was thinking how much I loved living in a place that embraced all of humanity.

One of the old-timers suggested gratitude as the topic. The discussion passed calmly from member to member, but the chairperson was becoming noticeably agitated. I glanced to the back of the room and discovered the source of his discomfort. An odd-looking man in his early 20s was drifting in and out of the door. The young homeless man—dressed in a bizarre combination of coveralls, tie-dyed T-shirt and an ill-fitting dress—would walk in, pour himself a cup of coffee, add copious amounts of sugar, grab a few cookies and then wander out. From his demeanor and behavior it was obvious he was suffering from mental illness.

Finally, the chairperson had enough of the young man's actions. "Get the hell out of here and don't come back," the chairman yelled at the interloper. "Who do you think you are, drinking our coffee and eating our cookies!" The young man put down his coffee and walked out. The room fell silent. The older woman put down her knitting and said, "I'm Joan and I'm an alcoholic." She related a story about a time she was chairing a meeting and had to deal with a person who exhibited unusal behavior. Her message was clear—in an open meeting, as long as someone isn't being disruptive we have tolerance for those less fortunate than ourselves. One by one, others in the meeting echoed Joan's message of acceptance and love.

Not one person pointed out to the chairman that he was wrong to berate the homeless man. Each one simply told a personal story of how they had handled a similar situation.

The chairperson got the message. He stopped the meeting and said "Just a minute everyone." He went outside and found the young man and brought him back into the meeting. He looked the rather embarrassed homeless guy straight in the eye and quietly said, "I'm sorry I yelled at you. I was wrong. Let me pour you a cup of coffee."

That incident happened almost 25 years ago, but the memory of that amends and the power of the group sharing their experience, strength, unity and hope has never left me.

Karen W.
Anderson, Indiana

Spot Check on I-94
October 2020

W e were due at the birthday party in just a few minutes. We were almost always late to parties, but we had to be early for this one because we were hosting. I hadn't looked at my GPS directions to the party venue until the car ride was already underway. "Turn right when you exit the interstate," it announced, or so I thought.

"Look for street numbers," I said to the carload of fourth-grade girls and my son Silas, who is 8 and on the autism spectrum. He was experiencing the accumulated auditory overstimulation of riding with a carload of fourth-grade girls.

It took a half-mile or more to see a street number: 1360. We were looking for 524. "How long till we get there?" one of the girls shouted in her "outside voice." "This is boring!"

"It's probably about a mile and a half away," I replied. "So, like, 20 minutes?" she asked. "Like, three minutes," I said, and all the other kids laughed. I felt slightly superior to the entire world for a half-second until I noticed another street number, 1548, and another, 1560. The numbers were increasing when they should have been decreasing. I felt instant frustration, anger, inadequacy, fear. My heart rate was climbing. Under my breath, I muttered, "We're going the wrong [expletive] way!"

"Did you just say the F-word?" my daughter Sarah asked, shocked and surprised. "Well ..." I muttered. I thought about lying, a snap reaction "old Andy" used to do. But I confessed instead. "No one was supposed to hear that," I said.

"My dad just said the F-word. In a car full of little kids!" Sarah announced at top volume. "It's my 10th birthday, all my best friends are here, and my dad just said the F-word. This is the best day ever!"

"I said the F-word in class one time," announced the bored girl. I thought ... Only once?

But I couldn't rejoice in superiority this time because I was too busy visualizing ways that the party would be ruined now that we were suddenly running late. It didn't help that Silas was starting to melt down from the excess stimulation, and there was nothing I could do right then to help him. As though that weren't enough, I was extremely disappointed with myself that my daughter had heard me curse.

But right then, I got the buzz of a phone notification. I pulled over. It was a text from my brother: "I'm here," it said. "Where are you?"

"I went the wrong way on 94," I texted back. "Oh my," came a text back. Then another: "Are you OK?" followed by, "Like wrong turn or wrong way?"

"Wrong turn," I texted back. And somehow, at the U-turn I was able to stop and experience some perspective. Some gratitude. Some acceptance. A nice out-of-self-inventory of what my current situation really was. I realized that I was in the car with my daughter and son on a very special day. She had her best friends with her. More friends would be waiting at the party venue.

My wife Tiffany would arrive at the venue before I would, to check in, to set up, to greet arriving guests. She had done a ton of work already to pull this party off. We would still make it to the party by its scheduled start time, we just wouldn't be early like we'd planned.

Silas would have relief from the noise in just a few minutes and, overall, he's becoming more and more high-functioning. At parent-teacher conferences the previous week, a small group of educators told me Silas was doing so well in school that they were going to re-evaluate him to see if he needed special services at all.

My daughter was shocked enough by hearing me curse under my breath that it somehow made her day. She didn't remember that "old Andy," the drinking Andy, used to curse at top volume all the time. I'm sober now and sober is my normal; "old Andy" mostly stays gone.

And most importantly, this upsetting detour only resulted in a simple wrong turn, not something much worse. I wasn't driving this carload of my kids and other people's kids directly into oncoming traffic. I could be very, very grateful for that.

Yesterday is history. Tomorrow is a mystery. All we have is today. After running that spot check inventory today and deciding how to proceed, I determined that Sarah was correct—today was the best day ever. Because we both decided to make it so and oriented our outlooks accordingly.

What I've learned in AA is that all of us, every day, have the power to make today the best or worst day ever. And sitting here at the end of it—yes, today was long—I'd say it was challenging. It had some down moments. I could have done more, and I could have done better. But all things tallied, while comparing it to my own history and letting tomorrow's mystery fade into the shadows where it belongs, today was the best. Tomorrow will be even better.

The things we do affect others. Picking up her daughter at the party, one parent pulled Tiffany aside and thanked her for inviting her child. They had just moved here. The girl was new in school and a little depressed, discouraged. She didn't feel she had any friends. When she got that party invitation from Sarah, she got some hope and some healthy pride. And she showed up and had a great time. And we all had a better time because she was there.

Now that I'm sober, life is a two-way street. You make a wrong turn, all you have to do is turn around and head in the direction of your best day.

Andy A.
St. Peters, Missouri

STEP ELEVEN

Sought through prayer and meditation to improve our conscious contact with God *as we understood Him*, praying only for knowledge of His will for us and the power to carry that out.

———————◆———————

The authors in this chapter speak of enhancing their connection to their Higher Powers through meditative and prayerful practices that allow, as the anonymous author of the story "But I Already Have a God" writes, "a very real, powerful, loving presence ... that flows through me." And you don't have to be sitting in the lotus position surrounded by candles, either. In "Letting the Spirit Join In," Tom W. shows how meditation can be a part of everyday life, whether you're walking or doing the dishes. The message? "Being united in body, mind and spirit is spiritual; it keeps me sober." These stories deepen our understanding of the role our Higher Powers play in our own lives, helping us understand the importance of prayer and meditation as valuable tools to enrich our sobriety.

Letting the Spirit Join In

November 1995

Practicing our Eleventh Step develops my ability to do one thing at a time. At meetings, people are sometimes amused when I say that. One man told me, "That's ridiculous, everyone knows how to do one thing at a time." Later on, when I asked him how he meditated, he said, "I can't stop my mind from racing long enough to do that." That remark demonstrates the purpose of the practice.

I wasn't born with the quiet mind needed to meditate. I work hard to develop it. The problem with me is that I'm alcoholic and as *Alcoholics Anonymous* says, "we alcoholics are undisciplined." So the real problem is lack of discipline.

My first sponsor showed me that I couldn't wait until I felt better to work the Steps. He said, "You must work the Steps in order to feel better." And so my work, my new purpose in life, was cut out.

When I decide to sit still for twenty minutes, it is my alcoholic mind that has the ability to distract me. Distraction usually comes to me in the form of a thought or a subtle sensation, a twitch, or an urge telling me to stop meditating and to do something else. Quieting this alcoholic mind is why I meditate. Following through on a decision to sit still for 20 minutes—no matter what happens—is spiritual practice.

With the purpose of discipline in mind, and without regard to the results, I have a simple method that I use for meditation. Allow me to pass it on.

Before assuming the posture to meditate, I set a timer for 21 minutes (21 is a spiritual number). Next, I say a prayer and ask God, as I understand God, for clear contact. Then for 20 minutes twice a day, morning and evening, I sit with my back straight in my quiet spot, with reverence for the practice. With my chin held level and my eyes closed, I focus on my breathing.

The only thing that exists now is the breath. When thoughts enter my mind I simply label them as "thinking." I don't chase after them. On the out breath I say, "be done."

This is my formal practice of our Eleventh Step. However, I'm an alcoholic and when something is good, I want more; so I've learned how to meditate even when I'm not sitting in my formal practice.

For example, I keep rhythm with my footsteps when I'm walking. Doing one thing—walking—with my body, and paying attention to it with my mind, gives my spirit a chance to join in. When I pay full attention to what I'm doing, I'm meditating. I'm united—body, mind and spirit—with a singleness of purpose. This helps quiet my alcoholic mind.

Another example is when I do the dishes. I no longer view the dishes as an unpleasant task. I see them as an opportunity to meditate. In fact, I stretch the job out. I touch the warmth of the water. I listen to it's rich flow. While watching the formation of bubbles I feel a loving God. I concentrate on washing the dishes and not on what I'm going to do next. The most important thing is what's in front of me—now.

One AA member who frequents my home group describes mindfulness this way: "Wherever you are—be there." Likewise: "When I walk, I walk; when I do dishes, I do dishes." You'd be amazed at the opportunities that are given for meditation during a 24 hour period. Being united in body, mind and spirit is spiritual; it keeps me sober.

Tom W.
Buffalo, New York

But I Already Have a God
January 2023

When I came through the doors of AA in August of 1990, I had been a Roman Catholic nun for more than 10 years. Despite this, I had hit rock bottom. I was completely powerless over alcohol and my life was beyond unmanageable.

But I came to the program still filled with pride, arrogance and the

cocksureness that Bill W. writes about. I saw the word "God" throughout the Twelve Steps and was arrogantly pleased—at least you people
were on the right track. I thought, I've had 10-plus years of rigorous
religious training behind me. What could AA possibly teach me?

Yet I read the Big Book avidly and found myself on every page. It
was a huge relief to learn that I was not alone, that there were others
who felt, thought and acted as I did. But I took great exception to
Ebby T.'s suggestion to Bill: "Why don't you choose your own conception of God?" To me that smacked of idolatry. You can't just create
God, I thought self-righteously.

It took me a very long time to be able to get honest and ask myself a
simple question: If belief in God were all that is required to get sober
and stay sober, why hadn't that worked for me?

In my life, I had God morning, noon and night. In my religious
community, we prayed together five times a day. In addition, we
had two half-hour periods of silent meditation each day, plus daily
mass, spiritual readings at each meal and private prayer as well. I was
steeped in God all day, every day. So why couldn't I stop drinking?

The answer was very simple. In spite of being immersed in the concept of "God," God was not real to me. I had never once asked what
God's will was for me. I was too busy dictating terms to God. Yes, I
had taken my vows for life. I had given myself completely to God, in
theory. The reality was that I had not turned my will and my life over
at all. I had built no relationship with God, I did not know or trust
God and I couldn't imagine relinquishing control of my life to anyone or anything, especially something I couldn't see, hear or touch. I
fought surrender with every single breath. "God" didn't work for me
because I didn't let him/her.

Somehow, in spite of my arrogance, I stayed sober. I gave up just
enough control to allow this power greater than myself to remove my
obsession with alcohol. Over the years, I attempted to find a God of
my own understanding, and in my own way I succeeded. The fact that
I did stay sober is to me a testimony to the patience, love and good
humor of my Higher Power.

A huge turning point came when I celebrated my 20th milestone in sobriety. I wasn't cocky. I wasn't proud, but I was in awe. Twenty years is a long time. How much had changed—in me, in the world—in 20 years. I felt as if my Higher Power said to me, "You're right, 20 years is a big deal but now let's start all over again."

That moment was a second beginning for me in establishing a relationship with this power greater than myself. For the first time, I felt able to define God for myself, to really choose my own conception of God.

And I understood that I wasn't "making up" God. Rather, I was understanding this power in a way that was very personal and individual to me. Since my native language is English, my Higher Power isn't going to speak to me in French. In the same way, the God of my understanding speaks to me in ways that are custom-made for me—in words, symbols, occurrences, encounters, in so many ways that are unmistakably, clearly from my God.

Today I seek to improve my conscious contact with this power through many different forms of prayer and meditation. I have learned that I can turn anything into a "god" and so I'm always changing my practice and approach. By this I mean that if I sit in a certain posture, light a candle, play soft music, and then get an "ah-ha" moment, I can believe that that awareness came from the candle, the posture and the song. So I repeat those external rituals to try to make sure God speaks to me again. I forget that the rituals are just that—rituals—and that they are not the God of my understanding.

So, I press on. I do many things—I sit in silence, I walk, I talk out loud, I read, I use meditative music—seeking my Higher Power in many different ways. The common denominator is that I keep seeking to maintain conscious contact.

I am no longer a nun, but I remain forever grateful for the years I spent in that life. They gave me a foundation on which I continue to build. In the intervening years, my Higher Power has led me in a direction that I could never have predicted or expected. Through everything that has happened in my life, my relationship with the God of my understanding has deepened and broadened. It has carried me through many challenges and through many joys.

I don't call my Higher Power "God"—I don't necessarily call this being by any name. It is simply a very real, powerful, loving presence. As the Big Book says, it is "a new power, peace, happiness, and sense of direction" that flows through me. I simply know I am loved.

To those who came in feeling skeptical, I hope you remain.

Anonymous
Wilsonville, Oregon

The Crying Sky
November 2021

When I joined AA more than 30 years ago, the idea that I would find a Higher Power of my own understanding seemed unlikely. As an atheist, I had difficulty seeing how a spiritual program of recovery could possibly apply to me.

Over the years however, I have indeed had a spiritual awakening, which allows me to stay sober and to help other alcoholics, particularly those who are atheists, find a path to recovery using our Twelve Steps.

When I came to AA, I knew that I was an alcoholic and that my life was unmanageable. I also knew that I was insane, and not just because of my repeated unsuccessful attempts to control my drinking. "Bottles were only a symbol" says the Big Book.

Luckily, I saw that the certainty of my insanity gave me a backdoor into the Second Step and a faith that would work for me in sobriety. As I attended meetings, through trial and error I began to see that if I anchored my mind to the present moment, all my guilt and shame about the past and all my hopes and fears about the future soon vanished. Doing my best to remain in contact with my immediate reality relieved me of the bondage of self. That's how living in the present moment became my first Higher Power. Staying in the present moment made me more sane and less crazy. It also helped me recognize that my Higher Power could change, moment by moment.

The Big Book suggests using the AA group itself as a Higher Power if we're having trouble with the "God" concept. My wife, who is also a long-standing member of AA and an atheist, considers the AA group her primary Higher Power. She is unable to access any meaningful spiritual experience without attending meetings. She doesn't "use" the group as a Higher Power; it simply functions that way for her. She prays and meditates daily too. These are practices that, along with meetings, allow her to live a useful and happy life.

How does an atheist pray? I go through a mental process of reminding myself of the laws and principles most likely to pertain to me. For example, my Third Step prayer is this:

I've decided to turn my will and my life over to reality just as it is, renouncing the mind's judgments, belief, expectations and desires. May I be increasingly awake to the life flowing through this body, free from the mind's creation of self, with its little dramas, likes, dislikes, trances and delusions, as well as its imaginary time travel into the past and future. May the effort of concentrated attention to reality clarify my views, intentions, speech, action and work.

Including the word "may" is a handy way of generating an intention for that moment's reality.

Alcoholics in recovery share a fatal brain disease that remains in remission if we stay connected to healing energy and conform to certain principles. If I have a cut on my finger, it may not be enough to say, "May the cut on my finger heal." That cut won't heal unless I set up conditions according to principles of healing: keep the cut clean, don't reinjure the site and be patient. Healing happens if I conform to certain laws.

I consider the concept of God to be a form of poetry about these laws. The poetic device is called "personification." By that, I mean giving human attributes to something that isn't human. When the great American blues musician Elmore James sings, "The sky is crying/look at the tears roll down the street," he's using personification to express a fundamental human experience. For me, "God" is a personification of fundamental spiritual laws that I can choose to obey or defy. Over the years, I've come to trust that if I obey these laws, I get to stay sober and have a reasonably sane life that is often happy.

Every morning, I deliberately turn my will and life over to these laws during my morning meditation. I pray for the ability to recognize what these spiritual principles ask of me today and for the power it takes to obey them. Then I go on to acknowledge any ways that I may have defied the law with my false pride, fears, dishonesty, self-deception, lust, anger, greed, gluttony, laziness and jealousy. I look for where these defects of character popped up in my life yesterday. My continued sobriety depends on being awake to my wrong steps.

Why would an atheist pray? Because the process of prayer changes the person who prays. Prayer turns me into a different, better person. A better "me" puts out more positive, supportive energy. In that way, my prayers seem to have an impact on others. This better allows me to fulfill my primary responsibility as a member of AA: When anyone, anywhere, reaches out for help, I want the hand of AA always to be there.

Joe M.
Los Altos Hills, California

Trusting the Silence
November 1991

Sometimes my faith in a Higher Power slips. I look at the people, places and things around me and ask, "Is this really what you had in mind for me? Is this what I sobered up for? Is this all there is?" And I sometimes get the silent treatment. That's only fair. My mouth has usually been running overtime, anyway.

Who is God? I don't need to know. I only need to have faith in a power greater than myself. What matters is what works, not my opinion of what works.

It took me years to figure that out, years in which I did mental and emotional battle with other people's conception of God, years in which I managed only to make myself miserable, cringing or scoffing whenever someone mentioned Step Three or Eleven. It took me a while sober to realize that it's a waste of time to take God's inventory.

So I don't pretend to know God well. And I really don't claim to pray respectably. I say the words "Thy will, not mine, be done" as if they were magic, as if they could help me stop yammering so much to have my will done. My prayers are usually brief and to the point. "Help!" is one I use often.

Often in sobriety, I've prayed when I needed to meditate. I've yammered at God so much that God can't get a word in edgewise. (What I practice with people, I cannot help but practice with God.) To me, meditation is simply being quiet and listening for a change. It is buttoning up my lip—and my mind that yaps even when my mouth is shut.

Meditation is the path by which I cease being caught up in my own mental "garbage in/garbage out" recycling. It is the path by which I walk out of the turmoil, trouble, pain, depression and frustration that I create in and around me.

Meditation is when I learn to be a child again. Not a noisy brat, but a child of the sort I always admired but rarely was as a child—quiet, serene, loving, trusting, teachable.

To meditate means I have to become willing to sit alone in silence—and endure silence patiently. It means trusting the silence around me for a while, as if it were an answer I had long sought. This is simple but not easy for me to do. I don't meditate to hear God's voice inside me, but merely to allow some space and time for the awareness of something higher than myself to grow more strongly within me.

I began doing meditation when I gave up my childish habit of expecting God to part the Red Sea and save me from myself once again, when I gave up my spoiled-brat routine of expecting God to show me a burning bush to prove that God really does care about me.

Practicing meditation means I open up for spiritual contact before disaster strikes, before even the need for prayer becomes desperately obvious. It's the brand of spiritual contact with God that I practice early enough in the day that I have nothing to tell God and nothing to ask God about in prayer. Meditation is the only time when I can be absolutely sure that I am not running on self-will.

In the beginning, while admitting I didn't know the first thing about how to meditate, I turned my ignorance into a major case of self-confusion by reading various books on meditation and trying to follow all the guidelines they presented.

Then simplicity mercifully struck. I found I didn't need to learn how to meditate before meditating. It turned out to be one of those learn-as-you-go things—just as learning how to stay sober is part of staying sober a day at a time. Meditation is something like showing up on a new job I don't know how to do, only to find out that by merely showing up on a regular basis and doing what is placed before me, I'm automatically doing what at first I did not know how to do and was sure I could never do.

When I practice listening in AA meetings, I am learning something I can use in private meditation practice. It took me a while to learn how to really listen to others in AA, to have my mind solely on what the speaker was saying, instead of hearing only the part that plugged me into my own preferred thinking. What I do in meetings is called listening. When I listen alone with God, it is called meditating. When I can listen completely to what you have to say without having to change or criticize it to meet my expectations, then I have a better chance of being able to do the same thing with God the next time I pray or meditate.

The hardest thing for me to do is listen honestly when I've asked God in prayer for direction regarding a particular person, place or thing. I tend to put words in God's mouth—the ones I want to hear. After years of misunderstanding God, I've devised for myself a simple test for reliability in prayer: If the answer is the one I want to hear—or the one that lets me sit back amid my complacency, laziness, or fear and let someone else do all the work in solving my problem for me—it probably isn't God's answer. What God wants me to do is rarely what I want to do.

For instance, if I want to avoid or leave, God wants me to stay and handle. If I want to be understood or accepted by others, God wants me to try to understand or accept others a bit more. If I want to forget, God wants me to forgive. If I want to point the finger of blame at someone else, God wants me to see my part in creating the disaster. If I want to dislike someone because of a grating character defect he or she has, God wants me to see the same defect in myself.

Meditation not only helps me hear God and others better, it also helps me see how even the tiny things I do daily for others strengthen me in my ability to cooperate with God. For I am one of those hard-headed alcoholics who had to practice cooperating with others for a while to learn how to cooperate with God, so that "turning it over" could become almost as easy and often as automatic as not taking the first drink.

In the last year, I've heard more silence than messages from God while praying or meditating. At this stage in my development, I think God is trying to teach me something I could not learn otherwise about patience and trust. What I'm now learning is how to apply to myself a bit of Native American wisdom that my sponsor shared with me over a decade ago: "If someone comes to you who is hungry and you give that person a fish, that person will expect to get a fish from you every time hunger strikes. But if, when the person comes to you the first time, you teach her or him to fish, that person will never be hungry again." So the messages I receive during meditation or prayer aren't anything like a fish from God. Instead, the messages are like God's lessons in fishing.

Whatever I learn during meditation applies to me in my life, not necessarily to anyone else. The messages are usually what I need to hear at a particular time, whether I agree or not. For example:

Help yourself by helping someone else first.

When in doubt, be silent.

Grow where you are planted.

Anonymous

As I Closed My Eyes
November 2015

Comfortably sitting on one of several padded chairs facing inward forming a rectangle, I closed my eyes. I was at an evening AA meeting in New Orleans where I had become acquainted with many of its 60 plus participants. Arriving early, I had chatted with several of the group's members, ranging from newcomers to oldtimers. I felt connected with the warm fellowship of this special group. Someone then dimmed the lights, which further increased the welcoming ambiance of the room.

With a little time remaining before the meeting started, I closed my eyes and attempted some private meditation. In addition to the cool breeze from an overhead fan, the only other stimulation I experienced was the sound of conversations. Rather than seek to extinguish the incoming vocal sounds, I embraced them into my private meditative world. I heard a composite of happy sharing. Not so much any particular voice, but rather a chorus of human sounds. There were moments of more female sounds and moments of more male sounds and then they all blended into a sonata of humans bonding to other humans. It became rhythmic, pulsating from loud to soft sounds, almost stopping for a brief moment, then continuing on. I was instantly reminded of a scene in Modest Mussorgsky's tone poem, Pictures at an Exhibition, where the composer musically described conversations at an art gallery, including a moment when all the musical renditions of talking briefly ceased. Then the musical conversations continued. With my eyes still closed, I realized I was privy to a symphony of human voices. At that moment, I felt sublimely connected with my kindred.

This happed to me, sitting there in my chair in a meditative trance, prior to my AA meeting. I was blissfully absorbing the spirituality of human sharing—a wonderful etude to a gathering of my sober fellows.

Tom L.
New Orleans, Louisiana

Note to Self
November 2013

I don't know about you, but I must be constantly reminded that I can control only two aspects of my life: my attitude and my sobriety date. Maybe someday that idea will come to me as naturally as drawing a breath, but for now, it's about as natural to me as a cupcake is to a health nut.

With a fair amount of time in AA, I know better than to be a "backseat driver," but every once in a while, I'll shout: "Turn right here God!" I think I know what's better for me, and even crazier, sometimes I even think I know what's best for you!

Step Three is one of the most frequently used Steps for me, as are Six, Seven and Eleven. These are where I talk to my "driver," God, and ask for direction. I've gotten better over the years, thanks in part to my willingness to remain teachable, and a little trick I learned from someone at a meeting.

First, I read my meditation books in the morning to expel my "dumpster demons." I keep one at my bedside, one in the bathroom, one at the coffee-maker and one in my truck. To assure that I stay in "constant contact" with my Higher Power during the day, I use notes to remind me to seek him. In my truck is a sticker that says, "You Are With Me," sitting just under the radio where I won't miss it. It helps me to improve my constant contact. And to make sure, when I get to work, there on my desk, in front of my computer is the note: "Good morning, this is God. I will be handling all your worries and concerns for today. I will not need your help!"

Matt S.
Buffalo Grove, Illinois

Make Me a Channel
November 2020

I remember when my sponsor gave me an assignment for Step Eleven. After we reviewed the Step in our book *Twelve Steps and Twelve Traditions,* he told me to read the Eleventh Step Prayer every day for 30 days and develop a routine for daily prayer and meditation.

I had been sober for approximately nine months at that time. I was going through a divorce and I was an assistant manager of a sober living environment, but not fully employed.

During this time, I had visitation with my sons every Sunday for a few hours. Just about every week, my soon-to-be ex-wife and I would engage in a heated argument just prior to my visit with my boys, which created a cloud that dampened our visit. To be clear, the cloud quickly disappeared once my boys and I got busy visiting, but they could feel the tension when I picked them up and dropped them off.

But one day, when I made the usual call to my wife to make sure that we were all agreed on the hand-over process (the time the argument usually would start) something really strange happened. Without any forethought or plan on my part, I asked her what she meant by something she said. I was not being sarcastic; I really wanted to understand what she meant, and she could tell I really wanted to understand. As you might imagine, she was a little skeptical, so she was cautious with her response. I restated what she said and asked if that was what she meant. She said yes and I told her that we agreed. We did not argue. In fact, I have found that this technique works well with most people most of the time.

Then it hit me. The Eleventh Step Prayer was taking hold of me. The prayer says, in part, "Lord, grant that I may seek rather to comfort, than to be comforted—to understand, than to be understood." The lesson here is that prayers must be followed by action. The prayer taught me to give others what I want for myself, and then

I will receive. This is consistent with most things in AA. We have to give it away to keep it, we pray for the people we resent to have everything we want for ourselves and we sponsor others so we can stay sober.

Going through the divorce made me feel very lonely, but attending AA meetings helped. I eventually took a service commitment as a greeter, which required that I arrive at meetings early to greet people at the door. That's when I made another discovery. I noticed that I was not lonely anymore after the second or third handshake.

My conscious contact with God is the biggest thing in my life today. I am never alone. I have a friend who absolutely loves me as I am, but has the power and cares enough to take me to better things, if I let him. My only dilemma is who to thank. Do I thank God for bringing me to AA or AA for showing me how to develop a better relationship with God?

I told a very dear friend of mine in the program that I knew that God has been doing his best to help me, but sometimes I could not see how exactly. Eventually, I realized that God had removed everything that was distracting me (job, family, etc.) so I could focus. Left with nothing, I was desperate and had nowhere to go. So he put a few others in my life who showed me to AA. And it was there that I learned how to communicate with him, when I "Sought through prayer and meditation to improve our conscious contact with God *as we understood Him,* praying only for knowledge of His will for us and the power to carry that out."

Michael J.
Omaha, Nebraska

STEP TWELVE

Having had a spiritual awakening as the result of these steps,
we tried to carry this message to alcoholics, and to practice these
principles in all our affairs.

———————◆———————

The stories in this chapter describe the rewards AAs experience
in reaching out to suffering alcoholics just as other AAs had
once reached out to them. The story "Chain Reaction" encap-
sulates the purpose and meaning of Step Twelve, as author Butch
M. describes a chance meeting with the sponsee of a man he had
helped Twelfth Step. "There was no way I could have foreseen that
a meeting of two complete strangers years earlier would lead to
this moment," he writes. "We never know where our Twelfth Step
activities will take us and the people we seek to help. Here was the
second generation of that night." The Twelfth Step packs quite a
wallop—Bill W. describes its "wonderful energy." As the stories in
this chapter demonstrate, we not only carry the message of recovery, aided by our spiritual awakening, but we now practice AA's
principles in every moment of our lives.

My One Year Gift
December 2022

When I walked into the Northland Group in Austin, Texas in June of 1982, I didn't know what to expect. I was a tough guy from Staten Island, totally bankrupt mentally, spiritually and physically. My Uncle Abe, who was sober 11 years at that time, took me to my first AA meeting and told me there were 12 Steps on the wall. "Read the First Step," he told me, "and stop at the word alcohol—work on that." When I read the Step, I said, "Uh oh, here we go," but I took his suggestion.

On my third day sober I went on a wet drunk Twelfth Step call with Abe. The guy was bombed, and his wife and kids were crying. The guy was rambling. I looked at my uncle and said, "What are we doing here? He doesn't even know his name." My uncle looked at me and said, "I am responsible." The bottom line is Abe had the Twelve Steps in him, and I had a half a Step.

As I started to grow in AA one Step at a time, my life got better and better like they told me. Over time I went on hundreds of Twelfth Step calls with my sponsor Roy and other members of our group in my first three years in Austin.

The greatest gift I got was in June of 1983. Roy and I were sitting at the Suburban Group and the phone rang. I answered it and it was a nurse at the hospital in downtown Austin. She asked me if we could come down to talk to a man in the ER. I told Roy and he said, "Let's go," then added, "You answered the phone, so it's your Twelfth Step call."

Right then I realized that that day was my one-year anniversary! Overwhelmed with gratitude, I went with Roy to the hospital and we talked to the man. Wow, what God and AA did for me that year. A Twelfth Step call on my anniversary!

I try to always remember: We carry the message, and God delivers it.

Dick H.
Staten Island, New York

In Your Bones
June 2007

I remember waking up, dirty and sick, under a billboard near an apartment complex. Well-dressed men and women were getting into their cars to go to work. They stared at me with disgust and fear.

There were times I was so paranoid I'd throw myself to the ground when certain cars went by for fear that someone I'd wronged the night before might recognize me (I didn't know what I might have done).

I remember waking up in strangers' beds or in hotels I couldn't afford or at home in the afternoons on days I was supposed to be at work. I remember pouring bourbon into my coffee. I remember chasing after relatives in anger, even lust, and falling asleep, time and again, with my chin on the toilet rim.

I remember much I'm too ashamed to confess—even anonymously. There's much I don't remember, but I recollect enough to know that I don't want to go back to who I've been.

My first AA meeting was 26 years ago. I was exhausted, scared, skinny, ashamed, and aching. A group of smiling people welcomed me. Somebody asked if it was anyone's first meeting and I shakily raised my hand. In the time-honored tradition of AA, they turned their regular meeting into a First Step meeting and they told their stories.

For the next three years, I was part of a group, but not a very loyal part. My attendance was hardly religious. I took a lot and didn't give much back. I just wanted not to drink, but I was angry as all get out. I drove like a madman. I argued a lot. I even tried to throw a lawn mower through the house.

I was dry but not sober, and I didn't know the difference. Then I moved and stopped going to regular meetings. I clung to my 24 hour book, and an AA uncle would check up on me now and then, but I went to only a few meetings over the next nine years. I didn't drink, but I didn't get better.

Do you need to hear it? Yelling, violence, taking it out on the kids, infidelities, lies, remorse, and loneliness—but enough success at work that I fooled people—or at least I thought I did—until two teenagers had the guts to come up to me one day and say, "It's obvious that you're angry and depressed, but it would help if you thought about what it's like to be on the other side of your face."

That got to me, and at about the same time, a friend, Bill, Twelfth Stepped me into his AA home group. That was in 1988. Pete, the group secretary, handed me a Big Book and a "Twelve and Twelve," and said, "These are yours. We try to work the Steps."

So, every Friday night I meet with them at one or another of our homes. Every other week we study a Step, see what the Big Book or the "Twelve and Twelve" has to say about it, and then we share and reflect. The next meeting is a topic of choice, and usually Grapevine provides the lead. This means that every year we go through the Steps twice, and believe me, there's always something newer, deeper or fresher to learn as we get healthier.

How I've come to love those Friday nights! Something happens during the "quiet time" and the reading of "How It Works." A peace, a serenity, comes into the room. I'm in a space where my worst self is acknowledged, accepted and welcomed with the absolute faith that I don't have to stay stuck in it. I don't fool anybody and I wouldn't want to. It feels good to shut up and listen to a lead, to learn that we're all in this together, to see sins become stories that help and heal, to watch shame turn into compassion and misery into miracles.

The guys in our group have faced some tough stuff and weathered it sober: diabetes, cancers, addictions and suicides in their families, divorces, rapes of loved ones, job losses, deaths of children.

Time and again we've talked about how the program gets into your bones, into your every thought, word, facial expression and decision. A crisis comes and you somehow know what to do. You learn that each moment, each interaction, is an opportunity "to practice these principles in all our affairs." The Twelve Steps are medicine, reminders, practice, and review—sudden insights and inspirations that spill out into all we do.

So much that made us alcoholic lives on in us unresolved, festering, recurring in the same old patterns, expressing itself in emotional binges, intolerance, negativity, self-righteousness, self-pity and worse. It's almost as though the program says, "OK, you've got the poison out of your system, now let's get to work on what caused you to reach for it." That's what the Steps are for.

Only by accepting my powerlessness over alcohol did I begin to discover the powers that alcohol had obliterated: God, health, truth, love, nature, fellowship, humor, creativity and even simple daily kindness.

Recently, I received my 26 year token. I held it toward the light, relieved that I hadn't had a drink in all that time, but humbled by the lack of quality of many of those days. But most of all, I felt gratitude for Bill W. and Dr. Bob; gratitude for those kind folks at my very first AA meeting—and at all the meetings since; for the alcoholics who have taken the time to work with other alcoholics; for my Friday night group; and gratitude for all the millions of unnamed and unknown who have worked the Twelve Steps.

Jim L.
Barrington, Illinois

Chain Reaction
December 2020

It was a hot night and he was leaning in through the low window on the far side of the meeting room of my men's group. I was a few years sober and still in my "savior" stage of sobriety, actively looking for people to sponsor.

As the meeting was ending and the men began to circle up for the closing prayer, I saw the guy step back out through the window and disappear. I ran around the back of the building and "headed him off" in the parking lot.

I introduced myself and asked him if it was his first meeting, as if I couldn't already tell. He said it was and told me his name was John. He had that "deer in the headlights" look. It made me remember my first AA meeting when I didn't know what was happening and was afraid of everyone.

I did my best to try to help him feel more comfortable by sharing just a little bit of my early story. He began to relax and I suggested we go talk over a cup of coffee. I was thrilled when he accepted my invitation.

We went to a coffee shop and talked for over an hour. I shared more of my story and heard a little bit of John's. I wasn't able to get him to ask me to be his sponsor that night, but I would see him from time to time over the next few weeks and months, across our meeting room. Our eyes would meet, and we would exchange a warm, knowing smile. Occasionally we would speak briefly. I learned that he had gotten a sponsor and had taken the Steps, which made sense as he looked calmer and so much more relaxed than he was when we first met. I could see that his skin finally fit.

A few years later, my wife and I attended the anniversary of an Intergroup north of our hometown. All those people who hadn't gotten in on the planning committee early enough ended up being assigned as greeters. There was a veritable phalanx of greeters outside the front door and it felt like the well-wishes would never end. One of those greeters was John. We exchanged a real warm hug.

"How long are you sober, now, John?" I asked. "Six years," he replied. "It looks good on you," I remarked.

The following year we saw each other at the same event and it just felt good to see him again, even though I had played no formal part in his sobriety.

A few years later at the same event, my wife and I had just gotten out of the car at the far end of the parking lot from the event venue. I could see John in the distance, still doing his greeter duty. As we started off across the parking lot, a young man came toward us. He was young, in his 20s, clean-cut and with a confident smile. He was wearing a suit. As he got closer to me, he opened his arms and welcomed me with a big hug, saying, "Thank you." I'd never seen this man before.

"For what?" I asked. What he said next rocked me back on my heels. "For taking my sponsor to coffee on his first night in AA," he replied. I stood there looking at him. "How long are you sober?" I asked. "About three years now," he replied with a smile.

There was no way I could have foreseen that a meeting of two complete strangers years earlier would lead to this moment. We never know where our Twelfth Step activities will take us and the people we seek to help. Here was the second generation of that night.

When we throw a stone in a pond, ripples emanate from the entry point in the water. They progress outward, away from us. They continue on to the far shore, to interact with ripples from a stone thrown by someone else whom we may never meet.

I was brought into the human chain reaction that is AA in 1983 by a man who had 35 days of sobriety. I never met the man who brought him to his first meeting, but in a way, I owe him my life.

Butch M.
Santee, California

Home But Not Alone
December 2015

From time to time a few of us take AA meetings to members who can't attend their regular meetings because they're confined to their homes, usually for medical reasons. One day we got a request to visit a young man I'll call Jimmy, who was under court-ordered home incarceration. This meant he could have visitors but could not leave his house.

During our visit he said he knew almost nothing about AA and had never been to an AA meeting, but thought he might be an alcoholic. From home, he had discovered some online AA meetings and read parts of the Big Book, but he wanted to speak directly with some sober alcoholics, so he called our Central Office for help.

As we were sharing our stories and discussing how we had found a new design for living through the Steps, my mind drifted to those early pioneers in AA and how they stayed sober. I silently wondered if someone who would not be able to attend a traditional AA meeting and knew almost nothing about AA could recover from that hopeless state of mind and body while confined to a few rooms in his home. He was a prisoner of sorts, but at least in prison they often have group AA meetings, which this man didn't have.

After listening to Jimmy it was obvious he knew he was an alcoholic. He was clearly desperate and motivated to change. I thought about all the sponsees I had had in the past, and how so many had drifted back into their sickness. I thought about how isolated Jimmy was, much like the AA Loners out at sea. But those Loners did stay sober.

So I thought, why not? Why not give it a try? You don't need a big AA meeting in a comfy clubhouse or church basement to pass on the message. All you need is one person sharing how they got sober with another person.

Over the next month Jimmy and I met regularly. We began by stocking his toolbox with the Big Book, the "Twelve and Twelve," *Living Sober* and *Daily Reflections*. We talked about what the circle and the triangle meant. We discussed how alcoholism affects the family, and I noted that there is a program to help them too.

As we read the Big Book together Jimmy did the work required to complete all the Steps. His Fourth Step was honest and his Fifth Step thorough. When it came time to do his Ninth Step, he invited his extended family to his house where he could make his amends. Phone and email allowed him to reach out to others he was unable to visit in person. He started to practice our rituals of daily inventory, including prayer and meditation.

Watching Jimmy change throughout his awakening was the most rewarding experience I had ever had in all my years in AA. Seeing the relief he got trudging his road was truly amazing. His obsession to drink had been removed. No longer did he hang his head when he opened the door to let me in. He stopped mumbling and looking at the floor when speaking. He began to have honest conversations with his wife and children. He asked how he could share AA's message with others even though he remained confined to his house. He couldn't wait to attend a public AA meeting. He became grateful for all he had, even though he feared what the future might hold for him.

I don't know how this story will end. Jimmy remains under home incarceration awaiting trial. He has not been given permission to attend AA meetings, but he has received and embraced the solution to his problem, and is willing to pass it on.

As for me, I still get a bit teary-eyed knowing that even without 90 meetings in 90 days, participation in a home group, setting up chairs, brewing coffee or standing up to receive his chips, Jimmy is staying sober by not drinking and practicing the principles our Steps suggest. All of this came about from just two alcoholics sitting face-to-face with only one well-worn book between them, and a Higher Power leading the way.

Alex M.
Louisville, Kentucky

I Cried as Much as He Did
December 2019

I approached the hospital on a warm afternoon with a brand-new Big Book in hand. The book still had that paper cover of blue and yellow on it that some of us throw away immediately, so nobody will know we're alcoholics.

Anyway, I was going to see a guy that I kind of knew. I am an alcoholic at heart, so I didn't exactly feel like I was going on my own free will. My sponsor was using his usual "Jedi mind tricks" to get me to go do something I didn't want to do. "Go see this guy," he said. And so I went. Sponsors are pretty clever, right?

I am also naturally competitive, and I wanted to get there before any of the other AA guys he texted would get there. I wanted to be first.

The boring truth is that it was simply God, executing his will through me, as always. But I'm rarely smart enough or humble enough to look at it that way, especially in the moment. I usually notice God after the fact.

I don't care for hospitals. I don't like the smells there. I don't like the food and I don't like the silence. I do find it ironic that a setting as cold and dreary as a hospital has brought me some of the best memories of my life. Both of my girls were born in hospitals. And though I didn't know it at the time, they were the happiest moments I would experience as a young father.

At the time, I took the experience of their births for granted. I hadn't yet found AA and I did not know what an awakening being a father would be for me. I was still caught up in old ideas and fear. Children were pretty far down on my list of things to care about. Alcohol was always first, followed by all of the miserable benefits of an ego-filled life.

Regardless, there isn't a single sad photo of me in either baby album, even though I recall being there and being worried sick over just about anything that crossed my mind. But as they say, "Worry is an ironic form of hope."

So, following my sponsor's direction, I got to the front desk and a sweet old woman asked me where I needed to go. I gave her the guy's first name and a room number. She politely asked, "Do you have a last name?

I'm an alcoholic. I don't exactly deal in last names, Fellowship or not. Even my favorite brand of liquor went by first names only: Jack, Jim and Johnny. I wasn't going to tell her that, of course. Good thing a room number goes a long way in a hospital.

I wondered what I would say to this guy. Maybe I would make like a courier and just drop off this blue brick Big Book and run. I wouldn't even make him sign for it. I'd just roll. I'd tell him to get better and mention that I hope to see him in a meeting. That's service work, right? But like my sponsor said, "You're not going to break anyone. Just tell your story."

Fine. If he asked, I would tell him my story. But the guy was in the ICU because of alcohol. The last thing he needed was to hear me talk about how great life is because I took it one day at a time.

I think too much. But there is magic in hearing a good story. That's what I find so solid about AA. Whenever I'm in a meeting, it doesn't fail. I never hear a bad story.

Even when someone who is obviously still sick is sitting in a meeting and spewing absurdities, if I listen hard enough, the message of AA is in there somewhere. Their words remind me of what it used to be like, and that is the powerful stuff I need to hear in order to get through the day with gratitude, God willing.

The first thing I always look at when I meet someone with 24 hours are the eyes. How red are they? How big are the bags? How much have they cried? How scared do they look?

The eyes truly are the windows to the soul. And whenever I see someone desperately trying to get sober, whether for the first time or all over again, the dusty windows are open. Everything, especially fear, is out in the open. And the clock is ticking.

My favorite speaker of all time, the late great Sandy B., said it perfectly: "When the ego gets cracked, there is only so much time to let some spiritual help in before it starts to shut." He was so right. Physical health returns and the ego convinces the alcoholic that AA is not really that important. The "I got this" factor slyly returns.

This guy certainly had the eyes. We hugged. We sat down and we talked. And I barely remember a word we said.

My takeaways are less about words and more about feelings, especially when it comes to working with another alcoholic. That day,

I cried as much as he did. I said, "Me too" as much as he did. And I talked about fear just as much as he did.

I think what we shared in common the most was the fear of the Fourth Step, which involves truth. Not just any truth, mind you, but the truth. Like this 19-year-old heroin addict once told me in treatment, "Rick, your secrets will kill you."

It was my new friend's secrets that put him in this hospital. And my only suggestion to him, like my sponsor and so many other happy, joyous and free members of AA suggested to me in countless meetings, was "Just be honest."

I pray for my friend that when he gets to the Fourth Step again, hopefully soon, he finds the courage to write down his secrets and to honestly share them in a Fifth Step with his sponsor.

I don't have the words to describe what happened to me when I did it the first time. All I know is that my life has not been the same since. It hasn't always been easy, but it has been amazing nonetheless.

I don't know what his future holds. The miracle in my life is that this gentleman was definitely there for me. The power of AA is reciprocal.

I hope someday I can see my friend again and tell him that I had another spiritual experience as a result of our meeting. I would tell him that for that day and hopefully more days to come, he helped save my life.

I left that afternoon with a feeling that maybe hospitals weren't so bad. I just needed to show up ready to practice some principles and to have a good motive. I think I'll swing by there a little more often.

Rick T.

Queen Creek, Arizona

Inside Raymondville

December 2020

Recently, at an AA meeting in my area, I happened to see the Grapevine annual prison issue (July 2018), with the headline: "Free on the Inside." Wow, those words brought forth a lot of old memories and increased my gratitude once again.

My husband and I used to travel from Canada to southern Texas for the winter months from 2003 until his death in 2016. I've gone there myself a couple of times since he passed. I found that there is an amazing AA community in that part of Texas.

In December 2010, I was sitting at a district meeting in the South Padre Island/Port Isabel area, where I heard a speaker named David say that members were needed to help bring AA meetings into Willacy Prison in Raymondville.

I felt that God was touching my heart and saying in no uncertain terms that I needed to help out. I went up and asked the speaker if he thought a woman from Canada would be able to help. "Let's find out," he replied.

It turned out, yes, indeed I'd be able to participate. Before long, a few of us drove off together for Gatesville, Texas, to do our official prison training. A short time later, I started helping out with that prison meeting, which was called "Free on the Inside."

The drive from South Padre Island to Raymondville is an hour and a half long. We had some great "meetings" before and after the AA meeting, on the road to and from the prison.

Each week, about 50 prisoners attended the meeting. During the week of Christmas, we got permission to bring food into the prison for a special celebration. We stopped on our way and got milk and various sodas, as well as all kinds of delicious Mexican pastries. The milk seemed to be their favorite of the treats.

Without exception, each week the men thanked us a lot. Some even said, "God bless you" when we were leaving. The prison chaplain told us that he saw a big difference in the men's attitudes and participation at the other regular prison activities after they attended their AA meetings.

One of the biggest impacts of doing this kind of service for me was an increase in my own gratitude. That gratitude began with the sound of the gates clanging shut behind us as we went inside and again after we left. That clanging when we were outside again was my own special "free on the outside" feeling.

I will always be grateful for those years in Raymondville.

Helaine D.
Sudbury, Ontario

Who's Gonna Drive You Home?
December 2015

The band finished their last number, the bartender announced last call and we all ordered one last drink. Before it arrived, I felt a hand on my shoulder and heard the question: "You come here often?" I looked up and it was the lead singer from the band. Up close I realized he was a guy from my last home group. I knew he did something on Wall Street, but then I remembered he played in a band a couple of times a week. Embarrassed, I said something I can't remember and he said: "We've missed you. Are these your new friends? You get good advice here?"

I shrugged my shoulders, hoping he'd leave. He put his hand on my arm, leaned forward as he lowered his voice and said: "Who's gonna tell you when it's too late? Who's gonna tell you things aren't so great? You can't go on thinking nothing's wrong. Who's gonna drive you home tonight?"

"I'm all right," I said. "I've just had a few. I thought your set was over." But he went on: "Who's gonna hold you down when you shake? Who's gonna come around when you break? You can't go on thinking nothing's wrong. Who's gonna drive you home tonight?"

Before I could say anything he said, "I'm gonna drive you home in your car. My wife will follow in mine. I'll pick you up at 6:30 for the earlybird meeting at St. Peters." Then he waved to the bartender and said, "His tab's on me," as he led me out to the nearly empty parking lot. By the grace of my Higher Power, meetings and people like Jack from the rooms, that was my last drink.

It is said that a grateful heart will not drink. It also does not forget. Four years later, while driving to a shopping center, the song "Drive" by The Cars came on the radio: "Who's gonna drive you home tonight?"

As tears rolled down my face and dripped off my chin onto the steering wheel, my worried wife asked, "What's wrong, what's wrong?" I said, "Nothing's wrong, it's just that sometimes life is so good I weep for joy."

David J.
Cary, North Carolina

The Front Lines
January 2022

The man was sweating, shaking, almost incoherent in his pain. "We know how you feel," my AA friend told him. "We've been there."

I was so nervous I didn't know what to say. This was my first Twelfth Step call, and I was green as new grass. At just over 90 days sober, I was in a dingy room in an old rooming house downtown in the middle of the night. The scene was just like the well-known AA painting, "The Man on the Bed."

The call had come in at midnight. The groups in our town were enjoying the New Year's alcathon in the meeting hall of a local church. A couple of men from my group took the call and elected me to go.

"Take somebody with you," they said, so I grabbed an oldtimer from my group and off we went. The oldtimer griped the whole way about having to leave the party and about the neighborhood we were headed into. But he went, and fortunately he did most of the talking.

"Do you want us to take you to the hospital?" I managed to squeak out. The young man who had called for help just shook his head.

The call actually came from the man's girlfriend. She was afraid he was going to die. She stayed in the opposite corner of the room while we talked. When we were finished, we gave her our phone numbers and she thanked us. I never heard from either of them again. I hope the kid found the program eventually.

A few months later, my sponsor suggested that I sign up for our local AA answering service. I was flattered that he thought I could handle it. Most late-night calls we received were from drunks who got the "midnight lonelies" and just needed a voice on the other end of the line. Well I certainly identified with that.

One of the saddest men I ever met called during daylight. I took my friend Kirk with me to meet the man. Kirk was a big guy and that made things easier. We went to another dreary boarding house downtown. We knocked at the front door and the man called to us from somewhere in the back. We went in. It was the nastiest place I'd ever seen. When we reached the little dimly lit room in the back, the guy was piled up in bed with his TV propped on his Big Book so he wouldn't have to sit up to watch it. He was all alone in his misery. No, he did not want to go with us to an AA meeting, but he wanted us to come see him the next day. We declined. I heard later he drank himself to death. That certainly gave me pause.

Later, Kirk went with me on another midnight call. A man's brother-in-law asked us to help. Let's call the fellow W. He was a reporter, and over a few months I felt like I got to know the guy. We rolled up to the curb of a neat little house and the brother-in-law escorted W. out to us. He was drunk so we took him to the hospital.

God bless emergency room staffs everywhere. They deserve our respect and gratitude. After the usual interminable wait, they escorted the man to a bed where a tired doctor examined him. As the doctor did his work, W. moved and a half pint of booze dropped out of his trench coat pocket with a clank.

The doctor lost his temper when he saw the bottle. I don't think I've ever seen a doctor that mad. We were unceremoniously kicked out of the hospital! We went back to the neat little house where we had collected the man. His brother-in-law met us at the door and refused to take him back. I looked at Kirk and he looked at me. "What do you want us to do with him?" I asked. "I am really sorry, but I don't care," answered his brother-in-law. And he shut the door.

Later, W. moved to a town close by. He got help from the Veterans Administration and got sober. So at least his story ended well.

One Sunday afternoon a call came in and none of my buddies were home. We had no cell phones back then, so I went alone. Not a good idea, but it was daylight at least. The guy who had called the answering service was actually the buddy of the man who needed help, and the caller was almost as drunk as the man he was calling about. But this man was not at all interested in talking to me or anybody else. I found him in his dingy living room in a small house on the East Side. His tax refund check had come in and he had set in a good supply of liquor. As he finished one bottle, he dumped the empty into the large bucket at his feet and opened another. He had been drinking for a couple of days and told me, profanely, to leave him alone. I gave his half-lit friend the only advice I could think of: "Take his car keys." The main danger now was getting cut from the broken glass in the large bucket.

A lot of calls come in from wives, mothers and even sisters. The guy I can expect to show up at a meeting after I've visited him is the one whose wife is mad. That can get results. Fortunately, Al-Anon meets at the same time so there is room for everyone.

A lot of the calls can be funny in a sad sort of way. Well, sometimes you have to laugh to keep from crying. The silliest such call came from a fellow who my sponsor and I had to talk off a roof. That sounds a little more dramatic than it was, but just a little. A friend in the program was a little too generous and he let the man stay in the small tool shed behind the pawn shop he owned. He called me one night because the guy had gotten falling-down drunk and then disappeared. I collected my sponsor and we came over to search the shrubbery and that kind of thing. There was a fire escape from the back of the building up to the roof and we found the guy off to one side up there peacefully passed out with his bottle cradled in his arms. Somehow we got him down with his precious vodka and off to the hospital. My car smelled like that cheap vodka for some time, which made my wife terribly suspicious.

I do not claim any great experience with Twelfth Step calls. Once in a good while a man will actually get sober and have a good life.

Today a dear friend of mine, a miserable drunk (weren't we all!), was in bad shape and we made several trips to the local emergency room and detox ward. He was so jittery and restless that we had to keep a close eye on him. He simply could not sit down. He would just wander off. At one point I had to chase him down in the hospital parking lot. Another day we reached out.

While I am now unable to do the service I once did, my sponsor's adage about the Twelfth Step is still apt: "It kept you sober."

Fair enough.

Tom L.
Albany, Georgia

In All Our Affairs
December 2021

Compared to other geezers like me, I'm either blessed or extremely lucky. I truly believe my Higher Power got me sober. However, he always held off telling me why he did so. Now I think I've figured it out.

In my 74 years on this earth, I keep getting diseases and challenges that have so far not killed me. Along with alcoholism, I have had two major neurosurgeries for spinal disease, prostate cancer surgery and now, total hip replacement surgery.

Don't feel sorry for me. I'm leading a blessed life. My Higher

Power has made it very clear to me that the reason I've been given this gift of longevity is so I can share my experiences with others. Does that sound a bit weird?

Six years ago, when I was lying on the operating room table at the cancer center, waiting for my prostate surgery, I asked my Higher Power to tell me why he gave me cancer. A month later I was in a prostate cancer survivor group sharing my experience with other cancer patients. It became clear to me that by using what I learned in my AA program, I was able to help other cancer patients as well as myself. The other cancer survivors were at first in awe of my "brilliance and expertise," as I came up with such unheard-of ideas as getting a "cancer sponsor," making a "gratitude list," doing service in the cancer survivor group and reaching out and helping other cancer patients. These actions work in our AA groups, so why couldn't they be used by cancer patients?

Until I broke my anonymity and told the cancer group about my alcoholism, none of them knew about any Twelve Step recovery programs. From then on, I've told everyone I have met in my cancer recovery about my alcoholism and asked them to call me if they need any help dealing with cancer, especially if they are having trouble staying sober during this traumatic period in their life.

I firmly believe that the Steps of AA lay out a blueprint in which the principles of AA, such as service, are applied to all our affairs. And that includes our health issues. The satisfaction I get from helping my fellow cancer patients not only keeps me sober, but it helps me deal with my own cancer. Who knows? That may be the reason why God has kept me alive so long.

The rewards I get back are enormous. Now that I have gotten my act together (well, almost together), I have regained the love of my wife of 52 years, as well as the love of our two wonderful sons, along with their wives and, especially, my five and a half grandchildren (it's a half because in three weeks we joyously look forward to the birth of another granddaughter in Nashville). My sons' wives keep popping out girls. Well, almost all girls. This latest birth will feature our fifth granddaughter. But we do have a handsome grandson living in California. I am most proud of the fact that none of my grandchildren or either of my daughters-in-law have ever seen me drunk.

So thanks to AA, I will keep sharing my experience as long as I'm able. How's that for in "all our affairs"?

Definitely Steve
Nashville, Tennessee

THE TWELVE STEPS

1. We admitted we were powerless over alcohol—that our lives had become unmanageable.
2. Came to believe that a Power greater than ourselves could restore us to sanity.
3. Made a decision to turn our will and our lives over to the care of God *as we understood Him.*
4. Made a searching and fearless moral inventory of ourselves.
5. Admitted to God, to ourselves, and to another human being the exact nature of our wrongs.
6. Were entirely ready to have God remove all these defects of character.
7. Humbly asked Him to remove our shortcomings.
8. Made a list of all persons we had harmed, and became willing to make amends to them all.
9. Made direct amends to such people wherever possible, except when to do so would injure them or others.
10. Continued to take personal inventory and when we were wrong promptly admitted it.
11. Sought through prayer and meditation to improve our conscious contact with God *as we understood Him,* praying only for knowledge of His will for us and the power to carry that out.
12. Having had a spiritual awakening as the result of these steps, we tried to carry this message to alcoholics, and to practice these principles in all our affairs.

THE TWELVE TRADITIONS

1. Our common welfare should come first; personal recovery depends upon A.A. unity.

2. For our group purpose there is but one ultimate authority—a loving God as He may express Himself in our group conscience. Our leaders are but trusted servants; they do not govern.

3. The only requirement for A.A. membership is a desire to stop drinking.

4. Each group should be autonomous except in matters affecting other groups or A.A. as a whole.

5. Each group has but one primary purpose—to carry its message to the alcoholic who still suffers.

6. An A.A. group ought never endorse, finance or lend the A.A. name to any related facility or outside enterprise, lest problems of money, property and prestige divert us from our primary purpose.

7. Every A.A. group ought to be fully self-supporting, declining outside contributions.

8. Alcoholics Anonymous should remain forever nonprofessional, but our service centers may employ special workers.

9. A.A., as such, ought never be organized; but we may create service boards or committees directly responsible to those they serve.

10. Alcoholics Anonymous has no opinion on outside issues; hence the A.A. name ought never be drawn into public controversy.

11. Our public relations policy is based on attraction rather than promotion; we need always maintain personal anonymity at the level of press, radio and films.

12. Anonymity is the spiritual foundation of all our traditions, ever reminding us to place principles before personalities.

AA Grapevine

AA Grapevine is AA's international monthly journal, published continuously since its first issue in June 1944. The AA pamphlet on AA Grapevine describes its scope and purpose this way: "As an integral part of Alcoholics Anonymous since 1944, the Grapevine publishes articles that reflect the full diversity of experience and thought found within the A.A. Fellowship, as does La Viña, the bimonthly Spanish-language magazine, first published in 1996. No one viewpoint or philosophy dominates their pages, and in determining content, the editorial staff relies on the principles of the Twelve Traditions."

In addition to magazines, AA Grapevine, Inc. also produces books, eBooks, audiobooks, mobile apps, a weekly podcast, an Instagram account, a YouTube channel and other items. It also offers a Grapevine Complete subscription, which includes the print magazine as well as complete online access, with new stories weekly, AudioGrapevine (the audio version of the magazine), the vast Grapevine Story Archive and current online issues of Grapevine and La Viña. For more information on AA Grapevine, or to subscribe to any of these, please visit the magazine's website at aagrapevine.org or write to:

AA Grapevine, Inc.
475 Riverside Drive
New York, NY 10115

Alcoholics Anonymous

AA's program of recovery is fully set forth in its basic text, *Alcoholics Anonymous* (commonly known as the Big Book), now in its Fourth Edition, as well as in *Twelve Steps and Twelve Traditions, Living Sober,* and other books. Information on AA can also be found on AA's website at www.aa.org, or by writing to:

Alcoholics Anonymous
Box 459
Grand Central Station
New York, NY 10163

For local resources, check your local telephone directory under "Alcoholics Anonymous." Four pamphlets, "This is A.A.," "Is A.A. For You?," "44 Questions," and "A Newcomer Asks" are also available from AA.